Connell Guide
to
Shakespeare's

———————

Twelfth Night

———————

by
David Schalkwyk

Contents

Who does Orsino want to kill? **103**

Where does Shakespeare leave us at
the end of *Twelfth Night*? **114**

NOTES

Introduction

Twelfth Night was my first Shakespeare play. I saw
it at school when I was nine. I was mesmerised by
the figure of Malvolio in yellow cross-garters
appearing before a deep blue cyclorama and
especially enjoyed Fabian's admonition to Sir
Andrew Aguecheek: "you are now sailed into the
north of my lady's opinion, where you will hang
like an icicle on a Dutchman's beard, unless you do
redeem it by some laudable attempt either of valor
or policy" (2.3). Why these lines? I don't know. I
found them very funny, and walked around the
school saying them to all and sundry until one of
the older boys told me to put a sock in it. I knew
nothing about Renaissance theories of love, or
household economies, or social hierarchies, but as
a young South African boy I had intimations of the
relations between masters and servants and the
spoilsport rigours of Puritan attitudes to playing
and revelry.

Today *Twelfth Night* is considered to be
Shakespeare's greatest romantic comedy, the
culmination of a series of works that includes *The
Taming of the Shrew*, *A Midsummer Night's
Dream*, *The Merchant of Venice*, *Much Ado About
Nothing* and *As You Like It*. Written at roughly the
same time as *Hamlet* (1600), it draws from its
comic predecessors in clearly identifiable ways,
but it also looks forward to the more sombre,

emotionally troubled and troubling "problem plays": *Measure for Measure* (1602), *All's Well That Ends Well* (1604) and *Hamlet* itself. There is no evidence that *Twelfth Night* was especially popular in Shakespeare's day, or in the 18th century. Dr Johnson complained that it rendered "no just picture of life", though he conceded it to be "exquisitely humorous". William Hazlitt, however, thought it Shakespeare's consummate, quintessential comedy, as did the Victorian editor, James Halliwell, who called it "the chief monument of the author's genius for Comedy, and the most perfect composition of its kind in the English or any other language". Many modern critics agree. "*Twelfth Night* is surely the greatest of all Shakespeare's pure comedies," says Harold Bloom, while another American academic, Stephen Booth, judges it to be "one of the most beautiful man-made things in the world". In it, claims Mary Beth Rose, Shakespeare "completely masters and exhausts this form of drama".

The mastery and the exhaustion are equally important. With *Twelfth Night* Shakespeare achieved an unmatched blend of plot and subplot, erotic lyricism and festive laughter, edgy satire and romantic melancholy. But he also suggests that the social and personal tensions that comedy is supposed to resolve cannot easily be dispatched in a "happy ending". With its main plot involving unrequited desire and loss of identity, and its parallel sub-plot of household jealousy and cruel gulling, *Twelfth Night* is as multi-faceted as any well-cut jewel. It is no wonder critics have disagreed about it so vehemently.

A summary of the plot

Act One

Duke Orsino has convinced himself that he is in love with the Countess Olivia, whose father and brother have both recently died. Meanwhile, Viola is shipwrecked on the coast of Illyria but, with the help of the ship's captain, makes it to the shore. Her twin brother, Sebastian, has disappeared. She believes him to be dead. Disguising herself as a young man named Cesario, and with the captain's help, she joins Orsino's household as a servant. Olivia refuses to see the duke – she says she will see no suitor for seven years while she mourns the loss of her brother. Orsino asks 'Cesario' to go and see Olivia on his behalf, and tell her of his passionate love.

Viola goes, though unwillingly because she herself has already fallen in love – at first sight – with the duke. Olivia agrees to see Cesario and hear what "he" has to say. Not realising Cesario is a girl in disguise, she too falls in love – with her messenger.

Act Two

Sebastian, the twin brother Viola feared was lost at sea, has also survived the shipwreck. Antonio, the sea captain who rescues him, decides he will follow his new friend to Orsino's court despite the fact that he has enemies there.

In Olivia's household, Sir Andrew Aguecheek, a silly squire and friend of Olivia's uncle, Sir Toby Belch, is considering trying to woo Olivia. He needs money and the plan suits Sir Toby, who also needs money and thinks he can fleece Sir Andrew. So he encourages Sir Andrew to pursue his niece. While the two men are carousing with Olivia's servants, Maria and Fabian, and her fool, Feste, they are interrupted by the pompous steward, Malvolio, who accuses them of disturbing the peace of the household with their late-night revelry. Sir Toby famously retorts: "Dost thou think, because thou art virtuous, there shall be no more cakes and ale?"

Sir Toby, Sir Andrew and Maria decide to take their revenge on Malvolio. They convince him that Olivia is secretly in love with him by planting a love letter, written by Maria in Olivia's hand. It asks Malvolio to wear yellow stockings cross-gartered, to be rude to the rest of the servants, and to smile constantly in the presence of Olivia. Malvolio finds the letter and reacts in surprised delight.

Act Three

Sebastian and Antonio arrive in Illyria. Sebastian decides to look around but Antonio, fearful of his enemies, heads for a lodging house called "The Elephant". Antonio gives Sebastian his purse and the two part. In Olivia's household, Malvolio behaves exactly as the letter instructs him and makes a fool of himself in front of his mistress. Olivia is shocked by the change in him and leaves him to his tormentors. Sir Andrew, meanwhile – after seeing Olivia showing affection to Cesario – is persuaded to challenge Cesario to a duel. They get as far as drawing their weapons on each other, but then Antonio arrives, prepared to fight on Cesario's behalf. (Confused by the disguise, he thinks Cesario is his friend Sebastian.) The fight is stopped but the officers who stop it recognise Antonio and take him into custody. Antonio asks Cesario for his purse back, still thinking Cesario is Sebastian. When Cesario can't oblige, Antonio thinks he has been betrayed.

Act IV
The confusion continues when Olivia meets Sebastian. Fooled, like Antonio, by the similarity of the two she takes him for Cesario and proposes to him. Sebastian is astonished by the proposal – coming, as it does, from a woman he has never met – but the two agree to a secret marriage. Malvolio, now in a darkened room, is teased mercilessly by Feste, disguised as a priest, who tries to persuade the steward that he is mad. Sir Toby, worried that he will only get into deeper trouble with Olivia, eventually puts a stop to the teasing.

Act V

In the final act, just one scene, Orsino confronts Antonio, whom he accuses of piracy. Antonio in turn accuses Cesario (still thinking Cesario is Sebastian) of betraying him by refusing to return his purse. The confusion becomes deeper when Olivia enters. She also mistakes Cesario for Sebastian, her new husband, and accuses Cesario of betraying her too. Olivia once again rejects Orsino, who rages against her and then directs his rage at Viola, still disguised as Cesario. Viola immediately says she is prepared to die for Orsino and declares her love for him.

The confusion is resolved when Sebastian himself enters. The duke asks Cesario, now revealed as Viola, to marry him. We learn that Sir Toby has married the servant, Maria. Antonio is left without a partner as Sebastian is reconciled with his new wife, Olivia. Malvolio exits, swearing revenge on his tormentors but Orsino sends Fabian to console him.

What is *Twelfth Night* about?

In the first recorded response to the play, after a performance at the Inns of Court in London in 1602, John Manningham, a law student in his late twenties, noted the play's historical, generic debts to the Roman dramatist Plautus and the Italian

Renaissance comedy of sexual deception, *Gl'Ingannati*. To modern eyes, what is strange about Manningham's view is that it ignores the romantic love plot entirely and records the gulling of Malvolio as the play's most memorable feature:

> A good practice in it to make the steward believe his lady-widow was in love with him... telling him what she likes best in him and prescribing his gesture, in smiling, his apparel, etc. and then, when he came to practice, making him believe they took him to be mad.

By the middle of the 18th century attention had shifted to the romantic plot, even though some regarded its resolution as "highly improbable", especially the play's defiance of differences of rank and station.

If we regard *Twelfth Night* as being primarily

SOURCES

The most immediate and direct source was probably a story by Barnaby Riche published 20 years earlier. *Riche his Farewell to Military Profession* is also about twins though they are not identical: a shipwrecked girl serves a young duke disguised as a boy and courts, on his behalf, a noble lady. The lady falls in love with the girl and then marries his twin brother by mistake. Riche's narrative sets out to show how lovers drink from "the cup of error":

> for to love them that hate us, to follow them that fly from us, to fawn on them

about love, and more particularly about the curious way in which we "fall" for other people while knowing virtually nothing about them, we will have grasped the central dramatic issue, though reducing the play to a simple formula fails to do justice to its richly complex mood and tone. Bruce Smith, one of *Twelfth Night*'s best critics, argues that it above all engages our imagination: "[It] is replete with moments in which visual sensation and sounds hover between sensuous numinousness and semantic specificity." What we experience indistinctly with our senses or through our imaginations when we watch and listen to it lies beyond the power of words fully to explain. As its sub-title – *What you will* – suggests, the play concerns the desires or fantasies or wills of its various characters and also invites the audience to participate freely in it by following their own fancies.

that frown on us, to curry favour with them that disdain us... who will not confess this to be an erroneous love, neither grounded upon wit nor reason?

It has been suggested this sentence may have inspired Shakespeare: Olivia echoes its phrasing in her declararion of love for Cesario: "Nor wit nor reason can my passion hide" (3.1).

Barnabe Riche's story is based in turn on two Italian comedies called *Gl'Inganni* ("The Mistakes") which in turn derive from an anonymous Italian play, *Gl'Ingannati* ("The Deceived") first performed at Siena in 1531. All three of these comedies contain the central story Riche used in his version and Shakespeare dramatised in *Twelfth Night* ∎

Shakespeare's romantic comedies usually begin with some kind of conflict and end with the resolution of that conflict. The conflict arises out of thwarted, mutual erotic desire between a young man and a woman. In Greek New Comedy, after which many of Shakespeare's comedies, like *A Midsummer Night's Dream* and *The Two Gentlemen of Verona*, are patterned, the desire of the romantic couple for each other is thwarted by the prohibition of an older figure of authority, usually the father of the young woman.

In *A Midsummer Night's Dream*, Hermia's love for Lysander is prohibited by her father, Egeus, who wants to force her to marry Demetrius, the man she hates. This prohibition is endorsed by another patriarchal figure of authority, Duke Theseus, who declares that he may not bend the laws of Athens, which determine that Hermia must follow her father's desire or else live her life in eternal chastity as a nun; or if she refuses either of those, "to die the death". It is only by fleeing into the erotic confusion of the woods, where Athenian authority is replaced by much darker possibilities, that everyone's desires can be accommodated so that the initial conflict can end with each couple getting what it wants.

This pattern involves an escape from the "normal" world of authority and prohibition into what is often called a "green world". This alternative world, in Northrop Frye's view, allows traditional authority to be temporarily lifted and conflicting desires accommodated – and "the device in the plot that brings hero and heroine together causes a new society to crystallise around the hero". It is the central mechanism whereby comedy achieves its essentially *social* ends.

The movement into a different, more fluid and more disorienting "green" world echoes the rituals of contemporary popular or folk festivals. The critic C.L. Barber argues that Shakespearean comedy incorporates aspects of these carnivalesque festivities – not only in the form of fools and clowns but also in the way the comedies are structured, with the protagonists having to *lose themselves to find themselves.* By giving temporary imaginative reign to their unruly desires and disordered impulses, the characters in *Twelfth Night* gain "clarification through release" (as, perhaps, does the audience too). Losing their identities and secure sense of selves in the initial conflict of wills and desires, they happily rediscover them at the end. So Shakespeare's young, desiring heroines lose their gendered identities when they pass themselves off as men, only to return to these identities in the end, when their desires can be fulfilled within the sanctity of marriage.

The conflict in Shakespeare's earlier comedies, then, tends to be generational, the desire thwarted usually being that of a young aristocratic woman expected not to have any desires of her own, and whose pursuit and expression of desire is seen as subversive of her father's right to use her as an object of exchange through marriage. As Theseus says to Hermia in *A Midsummer Night's Dream*, "to you, your father should be as a god..." (1.1). The comic structure of Shakespeare's comedies, however, allows young women like Hermia to pursue their desires without personal loss or disapprobation.

The predictable ending in marriage is celebrated by some critics but decried by others as an essentially *conservative* force. Barber's notion that comedy achieves clarification through release assumes that what is "clarified" is the superiority of the normal world over the topsy-turvy one, in which a purely imaginative release of inhibitions allows for the eventual recognition of one's "true" place in the world. The conservatism of this resolution has led some Marxist and feminist critics to claim that the inevitably closing form of comedy means that it finally endorses all the

THE TITLE

As Keir Elam notes, a title that is not directly descriptive of the main action, like *The Taming of the Shrew*, or of the main characters, like *The Two Gentlemen of Verona*, or of the dominant atmosphere, like *A Midsummer Night's Dream*, or even of the overall moral (*Measure for Measure*), becomes a "happy hermeneutic hunting ground".

Twelfth Night alludes to the carnival which ended the Christmas holiday season on the 6th of January. The play, says C.L. Barber, "deals with the sort of folly which the title points to, the folly of misrule" – that is, with the revels in early modern England which hierarchies of a patriarchal, class-based system: the aristocrats get to celebrate their desires within a closed community based on social hierarchy, and no matter how feisty or intelligent a young woman might be, there is always a man at the end whose marriage kiss "stops [her] mouth" and re-subordinates her to a new masculine will. And however much comedies like *The Merchant of Venice, The Two Gentlemen of Verona, As You Like It,* and *Twelfth Night* may flirt with the possibility and reality of homoerotic desire, as Bruce Smith avers, the plays always end by marginalising such desire: "Topsyturvydom has plenty of room for homosexual flirtation – but only till the Lord of Misrule abdicates."

The very notion of the "happy ending" of a comedy thus seems to be inherently conservative and exclusive, even oppressive. "Happy for

marked the last day of the Christmas season, and are associated in particular with the election of a "Festus" or "Lord of Misrule" to preside over the merrymaking.

The appointment of this mock king had pagan roots, evoking the anarchic spirit of the ancient Saturnalia. One of the central events of the celebrations was disguising or mumming (acting), later transformed into the court masque, which survived as a Twelfth Night event until the fall of the monarchy in 1642. In this sense, as Elam says, Viola's disguise is as appropriate as the antics of the revelers. "The saturnalian reading of title and play gains force from the oppositional presence of a 'Puritan' steward. Protestant fundamentalists reserved special bile for [the spectacle of] Christmas misrule..."

Twelfth Night, however, was also a significant date in the church calendar, the Epiphany, a feast celebrating whom?" is the question we should always ask. But having asked that, it is a mistake to put too much emphasis on the ending: a play is a combination of meaning and feeling always in motion – it is a series of dialogical encounters and events, a process. It releases disruptive energies and passions, desires and pleasures that cannot be squeezed back into the bottle by an often perfunctory and sometimes not altogether satisfactory conclusion.

Moreover, *Twelfth Night* differs from the earlier comedies in significant ways. As Joseph Summers points out in 'The Masks of *Twelfth Night*', there is no older generation: it "has been abolished, and there are no parents at all". The "only individuals possibly over thirty are drunkards, jokesters, and gulls, totally without authority". All the external barriers to fulfillment, then, have been eliminated

the revelation of Christ, and some commentators have seen evidence of specifically Christian themes. The play itself promises an epiphany, or revelation, and Barbara Lewalski sees Viola and Sebastian as comic types of the incarnate Christ, in the two miraculously delivered outside agents who will help cure the unhappy inhabitants of Illyria.

The events of the play don't actually take place on Twelfth Night and clues in the text suggest it is set not in mid-winter but in spring or summer. ("Away before me to sweet beds of flowers," says Orsino (1.1). "Why, this is very midsummer madness," exclaims Olivia (3.4).) Nor is the action confined to a single day or night, prompting Samuel Pepys to observe that it is "but a silly play, and not relating at all to the name or day". Pepys misses the point: the title should be understood figuratively. Shakespeare is signaling that "in what becomes almost a parody of the state desired by the ordinary young lovers, the Hermias and Lysanders – or even the Rosalinds and Orlandos". So a happy ending should be easy to achieve. Yet the inhabitants of Illyria feel anything but free. "Their own actions provide the barriers, for most of them know neither themselves, nor others," says Summers.

And the conclusion of *Twelfth Night* is by no means straightforward. Orsino , Olivia, Viola and Sebastian have their desires reshaped and fulfilled, but not everyone – notably Malvolio, Sir Andrew and Antonio – gets what they desire. At the end of Trevor Nunn's film of *Twelfth Night*, the aristocratic couples are shown celebrating in the golden glow of Orsino's palace while the other characters successively leave Olivia's mansion in a rain-drenched, autumnal landscape.

he is going to take the same licence to flout convention as Twelfth Night does. Kiernan Ryan writes:

> In this comedy, the title implies, we can expect the same topsy-turvy travesty of what passes for normality to prevail, but only for as long as the comedy lasts...

But *Twelfth Night*'s title also announces that "with this play the carnival is truly over": this will be the last festive comedy Shakespeare will write. Ryan thinks there is an air of "disenchantment" about the alternative title, too: *What you will* underlines Shakespeare's "playful intimacy with the public" but at the same time the ambiguity of the phrase allows him "to tease his audience by promising to give them what they want... while intimating that the play's satisfactions are not quite so predicable, and they must make of it what they will" ∎

Shakespearean comedy tends to exclude at least one figure from the concluding celebration: Jacques in *As You Like It*, Don John in *Much Ado About Nothing*, and, most notably, Shylock and Antonio in *The Merchant of Venice*. *Twelfth Night* multiplies the figures whose desires either run contrary to a sanctioned order or are not recognised by even the reconstituted and more accommodating society. In doing so it limits the inclusiveness of a purely comic resolution, and calls into question the traditional reach of popular festival.

Antonio echoes his namesake in *The Merchant of Venice* by having his love for his male friend displaced by heterosexual marriage; Malvolio, whose desire for upward mobility through marriage to his mistress is tormented and punished, leaves the stage in an utterly uncomedic spirit, vowing to "be revenged upon the pack of you"; Sir Andrew leaves empty-handed, duped and fleeced by his apparent friend, Sir Toby; and whereas Maria achieves her desire for upward mobility through her marriage to Sir Toby (which pointedly happens offstage and is not publicly celebrated), her advantage is questionable, considering Sir Toby's profligacy and drinking habits. Shakespeare is clearly testing the limits of the genre in his last romantic comedy.

Even for those who find their partners, the ending of *Twelfth Night* has what has been called a fairytale neatness. The whole comedy, says Kiernan Ryan, cries with Viola "Prove true,

...elena Bonham Carter as Olivia and Imogen Stubbs as Viola in Trevor Nunn's 1996 film adaption

imagination, O prove true" (3.4), but the gulf
between what can be imagined and what proves
possible is either demonstrably unbridgeable or
may, in the end, prove so. "We are seduced into
believing that the instinct for order in comic art
will always prevail over the anarchy of our inner
lives," says the playwright Simon Gray in a much-
quoted review:

> And so in a sense it does, on the stage – for
> there, after all, even poor Antonio, hopelessly in
> love with another man and with no substitute of
> the 'correct' sex to be flourished out of the cast

list or the wrong clothes, can still be made to rejoice in those flip and inconsequential pairings with which the play concludes. But still he lingers in the memory to remind us that Illyria is after all an illusion that has been fashioned out of much potential, and some actual, pain.

The extent to which this pain, real and potential, has been caused by arbitrary and/or misplaced desire is at the heart of *Twelfth Night*. If Shakespeare treats this in a sunnier way than he does in *Othello*, we are never allowed to forget how vulnerable the characters are and the sense that there is what the American professor Harold Bloom calls an "abyss" which "hovers" just beyond the play and into which the characters are in constant danger of falling. "Wild with laughter, *Twelfth Night* is nevertheless always on the edge of violence."

What does *Twelfth Night* tell us about love?

Twelfth Night is not merely concerned with love, but with ignorance and self-deception in love; in the world of this play, ignorance and self-deception are more or less *synonymous* with love; instantaneous and inexplicable, it makes no sense; it is a huge leap of faith based on almost nothing.

Perhaps love is just like that. "Shakespeare's acute sense that *all* sexual love is arbitrary in its origins but overdetermined in its teleology is at the centre of *Twelfth Night*," says Harold Bloom.* In his film of the play, Trevor Nunn begins not with Orsino but with the shipwreck, though Shakespeare had profoundly considered reasons for starting his play with Orsino and his languid meditations on love. What Bloom calls Orsino's "amiable erotic lunacy" prepares us for what is to come.

The Duke's opening line (probably the second most well-known line in Shakespeare after *Hamlet*'s "To be or not to be") conjoins music, love, and the casual power of aristocratic whim. "If music be the food of love", he commands, "play on":

> *Give me excess of it, that, surfeiting,*
> *The appetite may sicken and so die.*
> *That strain again! It had a dying fall.*
> *O, it came o'er my ear like the sweet sound*
> *That breathes upon a bank of violets,*
> *Stealing and giving odour. (1.1)*

The words sound wonderfully mellifluous and deeply felt, but the idea of love they express is troubling: Orsino is dreaming about a woman he scarcely knows and doesn't meet at all in the play until the last act.

He begins with a conditional (*"If... then"*) rather than a statement ("music *is* the food of love"). The

*Teleology here means that there is a design or purpose in natural processes which, once set in motion, can't be stopped.

grammar of his utterance therefore offers two different possibilities rather than certainties: 1) music *may* be the food of love (if this is so, carry on playing the tune), and 2) I *may* be in love (if that is true, then feed me music). Is the duke in love? He *thinks* he is. But his idea of love is strange. If music is the food of love, he quickly tires of it. One of the enjoyable comic ironies of this scene is that the speaker shows no sign of any real "appetite" for music; he talks through it, and, after naively demanding one "phrase" again, stops the musicians anyway: "Enough." The speech tells much more than the speaker knows. As countless critics have pointed out, Orsino isn't in love with Olivia, he's in love with love, like Romeo in his Rosalind phase. And when he expresses the hope that the "appetite" (for love) will "sicken" and "die", we are conscious that what he says may be what he *needs* but it is not what he *wants*.

The contradictions in Orsino's attitude remain in a later conversation with Cesario, when he offers himself as the paragon of true love:

> *For such as I am, all true lovers are,*
> *Unstaid and skittish in all motions else*
> *Save in the constant image of the creature*
> *That is beloved. (2.4)*

The duke's indulgence in the shapes of his own fancy make it quite clear, again, that he is in love with nothing more than his own imaginary *idea* of Olivia who, like the adored Lady in the courtly love tradition, is a compendium of generic pictures. Women in this tradition are the creatures (notice Orsino's use of this word) of poetically inspired desire. No one can tell them apart. Olivia is right to refuse to have anything to do with him.

More troubling than Orsino's indulgence in his own fantasies is his violent rejection of the capacity of any woman to love properly.

> *There is no woman's sides*
> *Can bide the beating of so strong a passion*
> *As love doth give my heart; no woman's heart*
> *So big, to hold so much; they lack retention.*
> *Alas, their love may be called appetite...*

MUSIC

In *Shakespeare and Music*, David Lindley draws attention to the contradiction between different conceptions in Shakespeare's time of the effects of music upon the human spirit: the neo-Platonic view of music, derived from the work of Marsilio Ficino, holds that music forms a passage which may unite human spirits and that of the cosmic *spiritus mundi*. The other, more mundanely Galenic theory, warns against the capacity of music to move the soul to baser passions and deeds. In this sense, it effeminises men and provokes idleness and lust. Shakespeare, Lindley argues, follows Thomas Wright, a contemporary theorist of the passions, along the middle way: the effect of music will finally depend not upon the intrinsic character of the music itself, but rather upon the nature of the listener ■

The pronouns highlight Orsino's infantile logic. In his account of the differences between men and women in love, he uses the distancing pronoun "they" of women and the inclusive word "we" of himself and Cesario. But we know that Cesario is actually Viola, one of "them": a woman deeply in love with Orsino. This knowledge evokes our sympathy for Viola, who is in effect excluded both from the conversation and from the capacity to love properly. We also recognise the trap that the deception has sprung for her, even as we know that without her disguise she would not be in a position to love the duke in the first place.

When Viola offers the hypothetical case of "some lady, as perhaps there is" who "Hath for your love as great a pang of heart / As you have for Olivia", she is talking about *herself*, but she has to adopt Orsino's distancing language. Provoked by the duke's uncompromising denigration of a mere woman's love, she first bursts out "Ay, but I know – " before thinking better of her impulse to defend herself. In Dorothy Tutin's performance in Peter Hall's 1958 production, Michael Billington described the words "as a soaring cry from the heart halted just in time and brought down in the vocal scale to a more moderate 'Too well what love women to men may owe'". The impassioned broken line, says Roger Warren in his introduction to the Oxford World's Classics edition of *Twelfth Night*,

is very characteristic of Viola. In her candour,

she cannot bear to hear Orsino going on about what is not true, and has to stop him even at the risk of almost revealing her identity. And the half-line emphasises that in her page's disguise she is frustrated from making the declaration of love she longs to make.

Disqualified from speaking from and of her own experience, Viola promptly invents an older sister, whom she can offer as a clear but fictitious example of the female capacity for faithful love, not merely fleeting desire. Notice how her pronouns continue to show her alienation from herself. She speaks of women as "they", and is forced to align herself with Orsino's male-centred "we" ("In faith, *they* are as true of heart as *we*"). This adoption of a fictional persona does allow her to suggest her love for Orsino through the conditional "As it might be, perhaps, were I a woman...":

ORSINO:
What dost thou know?
VIOLA:
Too well what love women to men may owe.
In faith, they are as true of heart as we.
My father had a daughter loved a man
As it might be, perhaps, were I a woman,
I should your Lordship.
ORSINO:
And what's her history?
VIOLA:

A blank, my lord. She never told her love,
But let concealment, like a worm i' th' bud,
Feed on her damask cheek. She pined in thought,
And with a green and yellow melancholy
She sat like Patience on a monument,
Smiling at grief.

The sister who could not speak her love turns out to be the embodiment of constancy, patience, and forbearance, all qualities expected of and admired in women. In contrast to the self-proclaimed male lover, this "sister" remains silent about her desire, and is consumed by her melancholy and grief. As Viola projects herself into the future via a story ostensibly about a sister's experience in the past, she figures herself as a carving on a tombstone, rigid, immobile, robbed of agency, and incapable of doing anything except exist as the acknowledged example of the self-sacrificial nature of *women's* "love indeed".

In one respect Viola and Orsino are alike. Love in this play does not arise from intimacy; it bears little relation to will or even thought; it is an affliction, something that just happens to us. But while Orsino sees himself as a victim – he can't help being in love; his desires pursue him "like fell and cruel hounds" – Viola's predicament moves us in a way that Orsino's doesn't. Her image of "Patience on a monument/Smiling at grief" is an image of what she expects to endure: she is going to suffer. Her speech is a fable of helplessness.

In *Doing Shakespeare*, Simon Palfrey

enumerates some of the effects of Viola's extraordinary words and their "delicate, reaching wistfulness": how, for example, the lines "internally" produce emotion.

> *My father had a daughter lov'd a man,*
> *As it might perhaps, were I a woman*

In the simple rhythms of the first of these two lines a *daughter* is "trapped" between the two men and the two verbs: between *father* and *man*, between *had* and *loved.* "The rhythms are at once hopeful and subdued, subdued and hopeful," says Palfrey, "a pattern repeated with a difference in the next line: *As it might perhaps,* she says hesitating, pausing on the conditional, before lifting optatively with *were I a woman,* returning to the previous line's litany of names: now she has said them all, or so it might seem: *father, daughter, man, woman.*" Then comes the risk, almost the recklessness, of Viola's closing half-line: *I should your lordship.* She is dropping an enormous hint here, pleading with her lord to see what she is saying, to look behind the mask and the costume and identify her as the woman speaking.

Orsino doesn't, of course, and we can infer his "emotional illiteracy" from his inability to detect the truth of what Viola is saying in his words: "And what's her history?" The word "history" both objectifies Viola's story and consigns it to the past when in fact she is talking about her experience "exactly now" and about the experience she can see all too clearly she will have in the future. Palfrey writes:

> The past and the present and the future are all one paralysed passion. So, Orsino's half-line both completes Viola's half-line and cues her next half-line speech-unit: 'A blank, my lord', which tartly encapsulates what she has become and what she will remain: erased, empty, veiled from sight.

But the word *blank* speaks of more than nullity. It sums up the pain of being ignored. Hence the two vivid vignettes which follow, each one suggesting movement but the movement being one of "hidden diminishment": concealment *feeding* on a cheek and Patience *smiling* at grief. The words reflect the same rhythm as the two lines discussed above, which also "both admit present paralysis and entrapment and yet reach uncertainly beyond it" (*into lov'd a man* and *were I a woman*).

While Viola thinks she will suffer she is not just a patient, grieving sister of stone. She is alive, active, flesh and blood, desiring and loving but also full of energy and determination. She uses her male friendship with the duke and her assumed male persona ("we men") to insist that her figure of female love loved, as she does, not merely in words but through her actions – *in deed* and indeed:

Was not this love indeed?
We men may say more, swear more, but indeed

28

Our shows are more than will; for still we prove
Much in our vows but little in our love.

Viola's speech moves Orsino, drawing him from his self-absorption to an interest in her and her story. "But died thy sister of her love, my boy?" Her famous response is packed with emotional implications.

I am all the daughters of my father's house,
And all my brothers too; and yet I know not...

To Roger Warren, this is the conversation, the moment, "with Orsino more interested in Viola than Olivia", which "makes it clear that the basis of their relationship and ultimate marriage is fully established". Shakespeare leaves us to fill in the blanks. If we don't see Orsino again until the final scene it is because we have no further need to see him; Shakespeare's stagecraft has done all that is necessary.

Is Orsino a "narcissistic fool"?

G. G. Gervinus, in 1850, seems to have been the first critic to pronounce Orsino in love with love, not with Olivia. In the 1965 Signet edition of *Twelfth Night*, Herschel Baker calls him "a narcissistic fool". Gareth Lloyd Evans says his "first speech has all the languid self-indulgence of a man [who lives] in an illusion of love". "The critics seem almost to compete with one another to find contemptuous labels for Orsino and to outdo each other in scorning him," notes Stephen Booth in his book, *Precious Nonsense*.

There is much about Orsino's character we are left to infer; he can be played in a variety of ways. Viola is far more intelligent, of course; in Shakespeare's comedies, as in Erasmus's colloquies on marriage, or even perhaps (ssh!) in life, the women just are smarter than the men. Playing Orsino as a fool, however, makes him unattractive to an audience while rendering Viola's violently rapid love at first sight even more inexplicable: we need to believe this is a good match.

He is undoubtedly inconsistent. Thus before his fatuous assertion to Viola/Cesario of the superiority of male to female passion he asserts

NARCISSUS

The emphasis on self-love or Narcissism in *Twelfth Night* was made explicit in Peter Gill's 1974 production, during which a large portrait of Narcissus dominated the set. Olivia's famous put-down - "O, you are sick of self-love, Malvolio" - also applies to other characters, including Olivia herself, who might be said to become infatuated with a mirror image of herself (in Viola), and, of course, Orsino. D.J. Palmer, writing about Shakespeare's debt to Ovid, says Narcissus is the play's governing Ovidian deity: Orsino's talk of how the spirit of love "falls into abatement and low price" echoes Ovid's Narcissus that "my plenty makes me poore" ∎

the opposite:

> *For boy, however we do praise ourselves,*
> *Our fancies are more giddy and unfirm,*
> *More longing, wavering, sooner lost and worn*
> *Than women's are. (2.4)*

But while he lacks Hamlet's brains and self-awareness, he shares with Hamlet a questing, speculative intelligence. A lonely dreamer with an idealistic cast of mind, his language in the opening scene is artificial but it is also, as Roger Warren says, full of vigour and immediacy and shows that he is "capable of powerful feeling and, most important, of development under Viola's influence". The ferocity of the image of the "fell and cruel hounds" which pursue him both makes real his frustrated desire and prepares us for his angry, homicidal outburst when he feels himself betrayed in the last scene.

Nor is he alone in deceiving himself: Olivia, too, is shown to be adrift from reality, as much in thrall to her melancholy as Orsino is to his love. Valentine, in the opening scene, describes her odd behaviour following the death of her brother. She will see no visitors,

> *But like a cloistress she will veiled walk,*
> *And water once a day her chamber round*
> *With eye-offending brine; all this to season*
> *A brother's dead love...*

Her self-deception in believing it is right and proper to mourn her brother for seven years and abjure the company of men is soon shown for what it is when she falls more or less immediately in love with Viola – in the guise of Cesario. Her love–sickness parallels the duke's, which has made him sad; she becomes sad too, using the word three times in a few lines at the start of Act Three, Scene Four. And Shakespeare makes the parallel between them even clearer when Viola remarks:

> With the same 'haviour that your passion bears
> Goes my master's griefs.

It is only when Orsino and Olivia come into contact with Viola that their behaviour begins to change: "her unaffected directness draw them from their affectations, and reveals the positive qualities that those mannerisms partly conceal," says Warren. Yet Olivia's love is not just remarkable for its suddenness – "How now?/Even so quickly may one catch the plague?" (the reference to "plague" echoing Orsino's language in the first scene) – but also for being the result of a deception, a fiction – a girl dressed up as a boy. "I am not that I play," Viola says, and "Poor lady, she were better love a dream" – which is the point. She does, like Orsino, "love a dream". Viola herself, however, has by now fallen for Orsino with unconscionable speed and with precious little knowledge of him. "Olivia is just as crazy as

Orsino, perhaps any handsome young man without aggressive affect might have done as well as Cesario," says Harold Bloom. Olivia, too, is unable to control her emotion, saying: "Fate, show thy force; ourselves we do not owe", with "owe" here meaning "control".

Just as the duke in *A Midsummer Night's Dream* compares lovers to lunatics, so in Illyria, love seems to be a form of madness. "Are all the people mad?" asks Sebastian when he is mistaken for Cesario in Act Four, and, as Kiernan Ryan observes, the answer the play gives to this question is clearly yes, with "all the people" including Sebastian himself. When Olivia makes her passion plain, he muses "Or am I mad, or else this is a dream" and concludes "If it be thus to dream, still let me sleep!" before surrendering to the situation and marrying the seemingly deranged woman he's only just met.

DESIRE

In their suggestive "dying fall", and Orsino's sudden withdrawal, "enough, no more", the duke's moody vacillations embody desire's cyclical process of longing and revulsion, especially in his rhythmical allusion to the dynamics of sexual orgasm in the procession of "surfeit, cloyment, and revolt". Shakespeare expresses this violent cycle of desire and disgust powerfully in his sonnet 129:

> The expense of spirit in a
> waste of shame
> Is lust in action; and till
> action, lust
> Is perjured, murderous,

To Jan Kott, in his controversial *Shakespeare Our Contemporary*, Illyria is "a country of erotic madness". One effect of the confusion which the play generates – the disguises, doubleness, mistaken and blurred identities – is, in a sense, to separate the ideas of love and desire expressed from the characters who express them. Orsino may be self-indulgent and self-deceiving but what he has to say to Viola about lovers being "skittish" is a view reflected in the play as a whole. Love causes the lover to act in fundamentally irrational and changing ways – but at the same time to transcend the basic unreliability of his or her emotions by maintaining the love object as an unchanging ideal.

Love is therefore paradoxical: it is both changing *and* constant. More important, the beloved is no more than a fantasy image that the lover projects upon the object of his desire. Stephen Greenblatt observes that "men love

bloody, full of blame,
Savage, extreme, rude,
          cruel, not to trust,
Enjoy'd no sooner but
          despised straight...

Renaissance philosophers of love, like Leone Ebreo, remark especially on this paradox of desire: "when we have partaken of it so far as to be sated then no lack remains, and at the same time all desire and love of such pleasure is exhausted, to be succeeded by dislike and disgust. So that desire and love are bound up with the lack of pleasure, not with its enjoyment". A female contemporary, Tullia D'Aragona, remarks on the same tendency: "Those who are moved by this desire and who love in this guise, as soon as they have reached their goal and satisfied their longing, will desist from their motion and will no longer love ... As a matter of fact ... they turn their love into hate." ∎

women precisely as *representations*". That means that there is an element of fantasy or fiction in all love, and Shakespeare's comedy embodies that fantasy. Writing about both *A Midsummer Night's Dream* and *Twelfth Night*, Terry Eagleton agrees: not only is it possible to be in love with love, he says, but "Shakespeare suspects that there is an element of this in all erotic relationships".

> What matters in the end is not whether characters 'really' love each other or not – since anyone can love anyone else – but whether their illusions interlock. If they do, if the illusion is total, mutual and internally consistent, then this is perhaps the nearest we can approximate to truth or reality.

What makes Viola so beguiling?

> "The sea, which is where the first accident that began the play occurred, is capable of supporting travel in any direction: so much the better if the person it carries has no fixed desire of his own, for he will always be satisfied with the result."

> Michael Witmore in
> *Shakespearean Metaphysics*

Viola comes from the sea. From the beginning she is touched by its allure, its vastness, its beauty, and its violence. (Her name, which alludes both to the flower which represents fancy and to the musical instrument, also forms the stem of 'violence' and 'violation'.) She is *Twelfth Night's* most enigmatic figure – possibly its most admirable character, she is also the centre of its deceptions. She has been saved by chance, the Captain tells her, and when she asks about her brother, Sebastian, the Captain's speech shows us how suddenly, and totally, things can change in this play's world.

> *I saw your brother,*
> *Most provident in peril, bind himself –*
> *Courage and hope both teaching him the practice –*
> *To a strong mast that lived upon the sea,*
> *Where, like Arion on the dolphin's back,*
> *I saw him hold acquaintance with the waves*
> *So long as I could see. (1.2)*

Simon Palfrey calls this a "classic Shakespeare sub-scene", reported rather than seen on stage. The ship has been split, the mast felled by waves or lightning. In a real storm it would have become just a dead, floating piece of detritus. But here it is alive: it *lived* upon the sea. It has not only endured, it has become "instantly habituated to the element, as though it was always of the sea". It has been transformed, just as Viola will be transformed. "In this world, evidently, you can enter a place, or a place enters you, and you are altered, touched like magic into new possibilities." Things happen by chance – "Ontology, identity, *home* – all these foundational things are creatures of circumstance, or indeed happenstance" – yet the changes that occur as a result are not capricious or random; they are in line with the expectations and hopes of the characters and, more generally, with the laws of Shakespearean comedy.

The "strong" living mast predicts what will happen to the "strong", masculine Sebastian: Sebastian binds himself to it: he grows with the mast and "holds acquaintance with the waves"; they become his home too. He turns into Arion*, the mast turns into a dolphin. It is as natural that he will survive as it is that Viola will fall in love with the most powerful man in the country where

*Arion was a mythical Greek figure, a poet famous for having been kidnapped by pirates and rescued by dolphins, and a symbol of the magical and redemptive powers of music.

ILLYRIA

The Captain's response to Viola's urgent question, "What country, friend, is this?" in 1.2 is not especially enlightening: "This is Illyria, lady." Viola suggests a punning resonance with Elysium, the mythical, Greek idea of paradise, where happy souls went after death, when she says, despairingly, "And what should I do in Illyria? / My brother he is in Elysium" (1.13-4). Leah Marcus observes that the name also recalls "lyric", a form of poetry that evokes emotions, especially related to love, and she has been shipwrecked.

Viola's first thought is to place herself as servant in the protective household of the ranking noblewoman, the countess Olivia:

O, that I served that lady,
And might not be delivered to the world
Till I had made mine own occasion mellow,
What my estate is!

Not only is she unsure *where* she is, she is also, at this point in her life, not entirely sure *who* she is. "In a non-trivial way, [*Twelfth Night*] is the story about how what happens makes you what you are," says Michael Witmore. It is "insistent in foregrounding the creative power of occasion and its foundational role in securing individual identities". The plays which Shakespeare was writing around this time show a growing

"delirium", a form of hallucinatory madness; Bruce Smith points out its relation to the stringed instrument, the lyre.

Geographically, Illyria was the ancient name of an area of the Adriatic coast, somewhere in the region of the present-day Albania and Croatia; in Shakespeare's time, however, it was the name of a series of city-states controlled by the Venetian republic. Roger Warren suggests Shakespeare might have seen Orsino and Olivia as neighbouring rulers of these city-states, though they seem just as much to be neighbouring Elizabethan aristocrats in England. Some interpreters see Illyria as simply a country of the mind. "The place is defined by the characters and the journey they undertake... which is an emotional journey," says the director Terry Hands ■

fascination with the nature of the "self". *Twelfth Night* suggests there is no real or essential "self"; the self is not fixed, but fluid: it is everything that we have in us to become, so what happens to us is crucial in shaping who we are. In this play Shakespeare is interested in putting Viola "on unstable ground", as Witmore puts it, and then seeing what happens when she attempts to cope with it. "She will not reveal her true identity in Illyria, but that identity will be 'delivered to the world' once she has 'made' occasion ripen or mellow."

The women in *Twelfth Night*, especially Viola, are both passive yet ready to take their opportunities when they come. "We ought to appreciate the paradox in imagining that Viola is simultaneously going to make something happen, and that that something is really an activity which she has no direct control over (the ripening of occasion)," says Witmore. Viola especially, but also Olivia and even Maria seem aware that their plans are what might be called "eventual":

> ...that they must hitch the wagon of their desires to the changing flux of circumstance if there is to be any satisfaction. In the Renaissance ideology of self-assertiveness, such a cultivation of chance was usually the prerogative of forward-looking males: only the bold man, aristocratic lore went, could discipline the goddesses of Fortune or Occasion and bring them to heel. The situation in *Twelfth Night* is

somewhat different, since it is often women who have the power to discern auspicious moments for action.

The combination of passivity and pro-activeness is clear in Viola's decision to become Cesario (as brave and reckless as her later behaviour when she hints at her real identity to Orsino). Critics have been puzzled by this initial plan to serve Orsino as a *eunuch*, with most assuming that this idea is dropped and not taken up again when the Duke accepts Viola into his service. Keir Elam traces the theme of castration to the Italian and Classical traditions of comedy. He argues that Viola's assumed castration is a powerful but paradoxical kind of performance that combines sexual self-denial with a powerful and irresistible erotic allure. As a castrato she becomes an erotic "blank", sexually disempowered but also a screen upon which others project their own desires.

Under her new name, Cesario, she preserves herself from the sexual attentions of men, but also prevents herself from pursuing her own desires, especially for her new master. She is new-born, as it were, through a kind of self-inflicted Caesarian section.

As we have seen, Viola's first thoughts in the play are about her twin, Sebastian, and, as Elam notes, one of the primary aims of her disguise "must be to keep her 'dead' brother alive, by way of a sort of talismanic magic". As Cesario, she can cease simply to resemble Sebastian and 'become' him, as she confesses when she hears Antonio name her brother:

> *He named Sebastian. I my brother know*
> *Yet living in my glass...*
> *For him I imitate (3.4)*

Viola's ability to imitate her brother explains her ability to take on a male role – and explains, too, why Sebastian can so easily replace her in Olivia's affections: "he is taking his 'rightful' place, usurped until now by Viola. Cesario is a point of converging identity between Viola and Sebastian". Or, as

TWINS

Shakespeare, says Keir Elam, may have sensed what modern research has demonstrated: that the death of a twin seems to cause a sense of desolation "different in kind to other bereavements", and the surviving twin often tries to 'compensate' for the loss by an attempt to assume the other's identity. Shakespeare had already touched on this theme in *A Comedy of Errors:*

> I to the world am like a drop
>   of water,
> That in the ocean seeks
>   another drop...

Shakepeare himself was the father of twins, a boy and a girl, Hamnet and Judith. Hamnet had died in 1596 and it's possible to imagine, as Kiernan Ryan says, that Shakespeare derived "a profound delight from dramatising what reality denied him: a twin son and brother's return from the dead" ∎

Northrop Frye has put it:

> In *Twelfth Night* the discovery of sexual identity is combined with the identical-twin theme: Orsino and Olivia are languishing in melancholy until out of the sea comes an ambiguous figure 'that can sing both high and low' who eventually becomes male to Olivia and female to Orsino.

Orsino assumes that Cesario's ambiguous figure will move Olivia – and how right he turns out to be. Her androgynous nature makes her sexy, attractive, and alluring to men and women alike. But Viola/Cesario is not attractive merely because of her deceptive clothes. Elam points out that her reference to being able to "sing ... and speak in many sorts of music" (1.2) means that her allure is essentially vocal. Lorna Hutson writes of her rhetorical attractiveness, of the beauty and force of her speech, which derive in part from her command of the civilised language of the new humanist values of education and decorum.

In Shakespeare's comedies *language* is erotic, and Viola speaks especially well, in all senses of the phrase. C.L. Barber remarks that "what enables Viola to bring off her role in disguise is her perfect courtesy". The music of her voice (much noted by Orsino in 1.4), her secure rhetorical command of the new discourses of polite, courtly speech and her fearlessness are not only attractive but *moving*.

Olivia is also poised, witty and eloquent: in a play full of doubling and parallels, the similarities between Olivia and Viola are striking. Both have a father recently dead; both mourn a 'dead' brother; both experience unrequited love. The sense of overlapping personalities is reinforced by their names: Viola's is virtually an anagram of Olivia's. (Malvolio's contains both their names, but opposes them with the perjorative 'Mal'.)

If Viola thrills us with her restless energy, her attractiveness is heightened by her vulnerability – as she walks the fine line between performance and exposure, trapped in the role that she has assumed – and by the dedication and loyalty she shows to Orsino, which wins him over. She fends off Olivia's approaches with perfect decorum, and is admirably independent, something many recent critics have tended to ignore. Her declaration of her constancy to Olivia is complicated by the fact that she speaks it as a man:

> *By Innocence, I swear, and by my youth,*
> *I have one heart, one bosom and one truth,*
> *And that no woman has, nor never none*
> *Shall mistress be of it save I alone. (3.2)*

The vow of integrity is paradoxically spoken by someone performing the role of *two* people. Who exactly is claiming to possess a single heart, bosom, and truth? Cesario, who speaks these lines, or Viola, whose voice lies behind the persona of

Cesario? And the riddle is compounded by the claim that "no woman" has the heart, bosom or truth, since each of them in fact belongs to the woman, Viola. Disguised as Cesario, she is at the centre not just of the play's interconnecting plots and conflicting passions, but of its subtle and witty exploration of the nature of the "self".

What makes the scene between Olivia and Viola so powerful and moving?

Viola may suffer her love for Orsino in silence, but as his friend and servant, Cesario, she displays a formidable agency and determination in helping him fulfil his desire for a different woman. Her insistence on remaining at Olivia's door until she is admitted to plead on behalf of her master by a drunken Sir Toby verges on rudeness, and she takes up her role as go-between with implacable energy. Intrigued by Malvolio's report of her unusual appearance and doggedness, Olivia relents, but only because she is inquisitive about Orsino's new servant rather than as a sign that she is ready to accede to his pleas.

If Orsino's notions about love are a predictably conventional set of humoural assumptions, the young Viola betrays her inexperience when she approaches Olivia with an equally outworn set of platitudes: the discourse of Petrarchan praise. Petrarch perfected the love sonnet in Italy in the 14th century, and his sonnets were brought to England by travellers like Sir Thomas Wyatt, who translated them into English and was instrumental in forging a particular English form of the sonnet in the years before Shakespeare established himself as a dramatist and poet. Shakespeare further transformed the sonnet from the innovative verse of Sir Philip Sidney, Michael Drayton, Henry Howard, Earl of Surrey, and Edmund Spenser by introducing an unreliable young man as the primary object of love and an unconventionally promiscuous dark woman from whom the poet cannot free himself.

The tradition of the Petrarchan sonnet involved praise by the lover (almost always a man) for the beauty and uniqueness of the beloved (almost always a woman), in an attempt to persuade the beloved to accede to the lover's desire. The beloved is idealised with extravagant metaphors and similes that celebrate her admired qualities. She is often broken down into various parts of her admirable body: hair like gold, lips like cherries, teeth like pearls, eyes like stars, breasts like melons, skin as white as snow, and so on. Over the page are two sonnets. The first, by Sir Philip Sidney, depends upon this Petrarchan blazon – the listing of beautiful body parts – while the second, by Shakespeare, is the most celebrated parody of the blazon.

In different ways, Sidney and Shakespeare both acknowledge the ways in which the poetry of praise *belies* the beloved, does her an injustice by not living up to her true image.

By putting sonnets or parodies of sonnets into his plays, Shakespeare gives them an embodied context: they are spoken by someone to someone else in an effort to get them to *do* something: to think or feel differently, to respond, to melt, to give in, to fall in love. Such sonnets are almost always as much about the poet as the person they celebrate. They are also *performative* rather than merely descriptive.

Cesario, acting on behalf of his master, is trying to induce a change of heart and attitude in Olivia, and, conventionally, resorts to the standard poetry of praise to do so: "Most radiant, exquisite, and unmatchable beauty..." (1.5). But Olivia has set a trap for Orsino's unwitting young messenger. When Cesario is finally permitted to speak to the "lady of the house", he confronts three or more different women, dressed similarly, and veiled. He does not know to whom to address the message. By confronting Cesario with a group of women who cannot be told apart, Olivia reveals the fundamental flaw in the poetry of *epideisis* (or praise): it might as well be addressed to any woman, because the terms are so generic, so undistinguished, so unspecific.

Olivia demonstrates that Orsino is not in love

What tongue can her perfections tell
Sir Philip Sidney

What tongue can her perfections tell,
In whose each part all pens may dwell?
Her hair fine threads of finest gold,
In curled knots man's thought to hold:
But that her forehead says, "In me
A whiter beauty you may see";
Whiter indeed, more white than snow,
Which on cold winter's face doth grow.
That doth present those even brows
Whose equal line their angles bows,
Like to the moon when after change
Her horned head abroad doth range;
And arches be to heavenly lids,
Whose wink each bold attempt forbids.
For the black stars those spheres contain,
The matchless pair, even praise doth stain.

Shakespeare's Sonnet no. 130

My mistress' eyes are nothing like the sun;
Coral is far more red than her lips' red;
If snow be white, why then her breasts are dun;
If hairs be wires, black wires grow on her head.
I have seen roses damask'd, red and white,
But no such roses see I in her cheeks;
And in some perfumes is there more delight
Than in the breath that from my mistress reeks.
I love to hear her speak, yet well I know
That music hath a far more pleasing sound;
I grant I never saw a goddess go;
My mistress, when she walks, treads on the ground:
And yet, by heaven, I think my love as rare
As any she belied with false compare.

with her, but rather with a fantasy figure, and by admitting that he has never seen the "lady of the house" that she is sent to praise, Viola/Cesario acknowledges the fragility of her position.

Olivia finally relents. She unveils herself, confronting Orsino's servant without her mask, and allows herself to be addressed directly. "Give us the place alone. We will hear this divinity." The conversation between Olivia and Viola/Cesario moves into a direct exchange in which Cesario's conventional and representative position is transformed into an unmediated engagement with Olivia.

Shakespeare develops the conversation by initially stressing its *formal* register. Viola insists upon her role as an intermediary: she has a part to play, beyond which she is not permitted to go – she is *Orsino's* agent, and she asks her hostess to follow the rules of politeness by revealing herself and listening to her message:

> *I can say little more than I have studied, and that question's out of my part. Good gentle one, give me modest assurance if you be the lady of the house, that I may proceed in my speech. (1.5)*

Cued by Viola's talk of having "studied" a "part", Olivia insults her by asking whether she is a "comedian" – a common player (like Shakespeare!). But she soon discovers that this young man will give as good as she gets. Viola/

Cesario pounces at once on Olivia's flippant joke – "If I do not usurp myself I am" – to remind her that she does not have the proper authority to keep herself from marriage, to which Olivia responds with an attack of her own on the conventional poetry of praise:

VIOLA:
  I will on with my speech in your praise and then show you the heart of my message.
OLIVIA:
  Come to what is important in 't. I forgive you the praise.
VIOLA:
  Alas, I took great pains to study it, and 'tis poetical.
OLIVIA:
  It is the more like to be feigned.

Echoing Touchstone's words in *As You Like It,* "The truest poetry is the most feigning", Olivia dismisses both poetry in general and the praise that it attempts to convey by claiming (in accordance with a long philosophical tradition beginning with the ancient Greek philosopher, Plato) that poetry and lovers always lie.

But it is when Viola asks the countess to reveal her face so that she can address her properly that Olivia wittily and coolly demolishes the poetry of praise and its chief instrument, the blazon. Viola appears to get the upper hand once Olivia

abandons the security of her protective veil, first
with a barbed remark about the possibility of
Olivia's using make-up to feign her beauty, and
then with a conventional *poetic* encomium to the
beauty revealed to her. The first terse, witty
exchange between the two of them is in prose,
before Cesario turns to verse, leading with an
elevated and far-fetched argument (also found in
Shakespeare's sonnets) that as the carrier of such
beauty, Olivia is duty-bound to leave the world a
copy – that is to say, marry and have children:

> *Lady, you are the cruel'st she alive*
> *If you will lead these graces to the grave*
> *And leave the world no copy.*

Olivia strikes back in prose by reducing the idea of
a copy to absurdity:

> *O, sir, I will not be so hard-hearted! I will give*
> *out divers schedules of my beauty. It shall be*
> *inventoried and every particle and utensil*
> *labeled to my will: as, item, two lips indifferent*
> *red; item, two grey eyes, with lids to them; item,*
> *one neck, one chin, and so forth. Were you sent*
> *hither to praise me?*

Olivia does two things here, both in parody of the
blazon: in opposition to the poetic notion that her
beauty is unique, she says she will promiscuously
circulate a catalogue of her features; and she

subjects the rhetoric of the blazon to ridicule by pretending that she is perfectly capable of listing those features, but in an utterly banal and bathetic way, as if they were an inventory of a kitchen: "two lips indifferent red" (compare the "cherry lips" of the sonneteer), "two grey eyes, with lids to them" (compare "two pots, with lids to them"), followed by the unadorned listing of "one neck... one chin, and so forth". The pun in "to my will" refers both to the kind of inventory of utensils and goods that would be contained in a will leaving possessions to inheritors and underlines Olivia's determined control over her own life through control of her own desires.

Olivia is free to mock Orsino's servant and to refuse his overtures because she is free from the control of men. The men who might have had some authority over her, her father and brother, are both dead and she can use her mourning for her brother as an excuse to refuse any visitors or invitations to love. Her mourning allows her to veil herself and withdraw from the outside world. Recall that Viola, behind her guise as Cesario, is also in mourning for a beloved brother, whom she (mistakenly) believes has drowned.

The two women, each experiencing intense emotions of loss and longing, now suddenly encounter each other on a different plane. In *Much Ado About Nothing*, the witty friction between Beatrice and Benedick is a sign of hidden sexual attraction or the very thing that leads to such attraction. As Stephen Greenblatt shows, it is precisely this kind of enticing friction in *Twelfth Night* that leads Olivia to drop her façade of mourning stand-offishness and gradually open herself to the strangely attractive young man who goads, praises and insults her in equal measure without a care for social hierarchy: "I see you what you are. You are too proud. / But, if you were the devil, you are fair." Olivia is moved by neither the supposed intensity of Orsino's desire ("adorations, fertile tears... groans that thunder love... sighs of fire") nor the social and personal qualities that make him a very good catch:

> *Your lord does know my mind. I cannot love him.*
> *Yet I suppose him virtuous, know him noble,*
> *Of great estate, of fresh and stainless youth;*
> *In voices well divulged, free, learned, and valiant,*
> *And in dimension and the shape of nature*
> *A gracious person. But yet I cannot love him.*

In an age when most aristocratic women were married off to men of precisely this stature and social rank for social rather personal reasons, Olivia is independent enough to insist upon a subversive idea that lies at the heart of Shakespeare plays as diverse as *Romeo and Juliet*, *A Midsummer Night's Dream* and *All's Well that Ends Well*: that love lies entirely in the eye of the beholder and is not to be persuaded by social or material attributes, no matter how "virtuous", "noble", "stainless", "free", "learned" or "valiant" a prospective lover may be. It sees not only with the eyes but with the mind, and latches on to the unique qualities of the beloved. It is this uniqueness that makes the traditional blazon so artificial.

Olivia is therefore not interested in what Orsino might do to show his love for her; but she is interested in Orsino's young man. "Why, what would *you* do?" she asks Cesario, who responds at once by moving into a new kind of verse – energetic, concrete, heart-felt:

> *Make me a willow cabin at your gate*
> *And call upon my soul within the house,*
> *Write loyal cantons of contemnèd love*
> *And sing them loud even in the dead of night,*
> *Hallow your name to the reverberate hills*
> *And make the babbling gossip of the air*
> *Cry out "Olivia!" O, you should not rest*
> *Between the elements of air and earth*
> *But you should pity me.*

Two things are happening here. The women are conjoined by the mutual depth of their loss – in their mutual mourning for brothers. And despite *Cesario's* insistence that he is acting on behalf of his master, his hypothetical vision of what he would do to persuade Olivia to love him is filled with *Viola's* passionate longing for Orsino. "Call Viola a repressed vitalist," says Harold Bloom, "alive with [Rosalind of *As You Like It's*] intensity, but constrained from expressing her strength." This elegiac passage, like the one she speaks to Orsino about "Patience... smiling at grief", is what Bloom calls "apotropaic"; intended "to ward off a fate that she courts by her passivity, from which she seems not able to rally herself".

The emotion is genuine, but displaced. How different is the direct insistence of the largely single and at most double syllables in "make me a willow cabin at your gate" – and "O, you should not rest / Between the elements of air and earth but you should pity me" – from the airy Latinate diction of her earlier, learnt lines: "Most radiant, exquisite, and unmatchable beauty" or "the nonpareil of beauty". As Harold Jenkins has pointed out, "the willow is the emblem of forsaken love" and those songs that issue from it are traditional love laments, but Viola's parody of these laments "is of the kind that does not belittle but transfigures the original", and Olivia "starts to listen".

We feel – and Olivia feels – a change of emotional gear in the way Viola now speaks. Notice the way in which the poetry conveys not merely indulged feeling, like Orsino's music that "breathes across a bank of violets / Stealing and giving odour" (1.1), but rather emotion expressed as action. It is what Viola would *do* that is emphasised, not merely what she feels. Notice also how Shakespeare evokes the music of Olivia's name and Viola's voice by the exact placing of polysyllabic words at the point where he wishes to evoke their insistent echo: "Hallow... reverberate... babbling gossip", before Viola achieves an emotional climax with the spondee, "Cry out" (//)*. This is then followed by the dying echo of Olivia's name in an iamb followed by a dactyl: "Olivia" (u/uu). It's as much the flexibility of Viola's rhythm in the speech as its poetic diction that produces the music that seduces audiences and Olivia alike.

Holding back only to assure herself of Cesario's parentage, Olivia allows herself to fall unrestrainedly in love with Orsino's messenger:

> How now?
> Even so quickly may one catch the plague
> Methinks I feel this youth's perfections
> With an invisible and subtle stealth
> To creep in at mine eyes. Well, let it be.

Shakespeare follows the traditional notion that love enters through the eyes and also that it is a form of sickness, but he gives his parody of the poetic blazon a further ironic twist. Now fully in love, Olivia resorts to exactly the language that she so denigrated when she thought it came from Orsino:

*A spondee is a metrical foot consisting of two long syllables. An iamb is an unstressed short syllable followed by a stressed longer one. A dactyl is a metrical foot consisting of one long or accented syllable followed by two short or unaccented ones.

"What is your parentage?"
"Above my fortunes, yet my state is well.
I am a gentleman." I'll be sworn thou art
Thy tongue, thy face, thy limbs, actions, and spirit
Do give thee fivefold blazon.

The diction may be conventional, but following Viola's passionate declaration, the rhythm of Olivia's speech gathers emotional momentum by following the expected iambs of "Thy tongue, thy face, thy limbs" (u/ u/ u/) with a spondee that echoes Viola's earlier rhythm: "Do give thee fivefold blazon" (/ / u /u /u).

Lorna Hutson is thus right to point out the attractiveness of Viola's improvisatory rhetoric, which moves us with its simple, direct beauty. Orsino does not – indeed he cannot – do what Viola does. It is how *Viola* would act, moved by her own longing for Orsino, that finally seduces Olivia. This is achieved by the musicality of her voice and the rhythmical intensity of her language. Viola's speech "is not a classic of romantic persuasiveness for nothing", says Simon Gray. "If it is ironic in its exaggerations, it is also insidiously enticing in its rhythms... and consequently the comedy in [Viola's] relationship with Olivia is both intensely erotic and dangerous."

What does *Twelfth Night* tell us about the nature of identity?

Modern critics make much of the atmosphere of erotic ambiguity in the Viola/Olivia scenes, and in those between Viola and Orsino. Stephen Greenblatt argues that whereas the "friction" of sexual activity could never be represented on Shakespeare's stage, the dramatist could convey such arousal through the friction of erotically charged, poetic language. In the end, however, despite Viola's disguise, the "feminine elements" in her body dominate. Consequently, "the 'true mettle' of her sex resolves the play's ambiguities by attaching Orsino's desire to an appropriate and 'natural' object".

Greenblatt's claim that Viola as a woman is ultimately shown to be the 'natural' object of Orsino's desire has drawn criticism from both feminist and queer critics, who maintain that *Twelfth Night* undermines any idea of a "natural" object of desire as much as it does the idea of a "true" identity. And it is undoubtedly true that Viola's acting like a *man* finally engages Orsino more deeply, at a level of real personal involvement, than his infatuation with the image of Olivia. There is something about this new young male servant that intrigues Orsino. Is it perhaps

TEN FACTS ABOUT
TWELFTH NIGHT

1.
There are various English as well as Italian allusions in *Twelfth Night*. For example, Viola's use of "Westward Ho!" , a typical cry of 16th century Thames boatmen, and Antonio's recommendation to Sebastian of "The Elephant": The Elephant was a pub not far from The Globe theatre.

2.
Malvolio is one of Shakespeare's most popular roles. Among the actors who have played it are John Gielgud, Laurence Olivier, Donald Sinden, Ian Holm, Simon Russell Beale, Derek Jacobi and Stephen Fry.

3.
The word "mad" and its offshoots crops up more often in *Twelfth Night* than in any other Shakespeare play. *The Comedy of Errors* comes second.

4.
The Danish philosopher Søren Kierkegaard opens his book *Philosophical Fragments* with the quote "Better well hanged than ill wed" which is a paraphrase of Feste's comment to Maria in Act 1,

Scene 5: "Many a good hanging prevents a bad marriage." Nietzsche also refers passingly to *Twelfth Night* (specifically, to Sir Andrew Aguecheek's suspicion, expressed in Act 1, Scene 3, that his excessive intake of beef is having an inverse effect on his wit) in the third essay of his *Genealogy of Morality*.

5.

Illyria was an ancient region of the Western Balkans whose coast (the eastern coast of the Adriatic Sea which is the only part of ancient Illyria which is relevant to the play) covered (from north to south) the coasts of modern day Slovenia, Croatia, Montenegro and Albania.

6.

Shakespeare in Love includes several references to *Twelfth Night*. Near the end of the film, Elizabeth I (Judi Dench) asks Shakespeare (Joseph Fiennes) to write a comedy for the Twelfth Night holiday. Shakespeare's love interest in the film, "Viola" (Gwyneth Paltrow), is the daughter of a wealthy merchant who disguises herself as a boy to become an actor; she is presented as Shakespeare's "true" inspiration for the heroine of *Twelfth Night*.

7.

Viola sustains her disguise longer than any other of

Shakespeare's cross-dressing heroines, maintaining it from the outset until the very end.

8.

On 14 May 1937, the BBC broadcast a 30-minute excerpt of *Twelfth Night*, the first known instance of a work of Shakespeare being performed on television. The production featured the then up and coming young actress, Greer Garson. The entire play was produced for television in 1939, starring another future Oscar-winner, Peggy Ashcroft.

9.

The British used to celebrate Twelfth Night with a drink called Lamb's Wool made from roasted apples, sugar and nutmeg in beer.

10.

In 2012, as part of the World Shakespeare Festival, the Royal Shakespeare Company presented *The Comedy of Errors*, *Twelfth Night*, and *The Tempest* as 'Shakespeare's Shipwreck Trilogy' both at Stratford and at the Round House Theatre in London.

his boyishness – something that Orsino highlights explicitly?

> *For they shall yet belie thy happy years*
> *That say thou art a man. Diana's lip*
> *Is not more smooth and rubious, thy small pipe*
> *Is as the maiden's organ, shrill and sound,*
> *And all is semblative a woman's part.* *(1.4)*

Orsino is talking about Cesario's throat and voice, but the suggestion of sexual organs is unmistakable. Nor is it clear whether the "pipe" is male or female. Perhaps, in her guise as a young man, Viola is paradoxically the perfect woman. Her overwhelming attractiveness arises precisely from her androgynous figure – neither male nor female, or perhaps both – which seduces *both* Orsino and Olivia. But it's not just the ambiguous body that plays its part. The person who inhabits the figure – with intelligence, fluency, and passionate dedication – is what seduces the play's characters and audiences alike.

Viola's cross-dressing achieves a number of different things: it endorses female desire and the emotional intensity that is usually confined to the "man's part"; as Lisa Jardine indicates, it conjoins adolescent males and women as equally powerless figures of sexual vulnerability and exploitation; it complicates the notion of same-sex desire; and it "exposes 'man' as a simulacrum and gender as a construction built on the faulty ground of exclusive, binary difference".

Other feminist critics echo this. Laura Levine says *Twelfth Night* brings to the surface deep-seated fears regarding the stability of gender distinctions and thus of the self. Catherine Belsey claims the play calls into question the very idea of a "true" identity. Shakespearean comedy, she argues, "can be read as disrupting sexual difference, calling into question that set of relations between terms which poses as inevitable an antithesis between masculine and feminine, men and women". Of all the comedies, *Twelfth Night* "takes the most remarkable risks with the identity of its central figure".

Marjorie Garber states that Shakespeare is concerned with "the double nature of all human beings, the fact that men and women all have something 'masculine' and something 'feminine' about them". She therefore directly contradicts the (male) critic C. L. Barber's claim that "the most fundamental distinction the play brings home to us is the difference between men and women". Judith Butler contradicts it too, with her thesis that gender roles are performative: being a man or a woman means learning to prefer certain things above others, to dress and carry one's body in determined ways, and even to speak in expected modes and tones. We are all brought up to act like men or women within a particular set of conventional social exclusions and prescriptions.

But against this it must be remembered that

unlike the figures of Rosalind and Portia, who enjoy the power they gain when they dress as men, Viola is constrained by her disguise or what, in Act Five, she calls "this my masculine usurped attire". Anne Barton says accurately that her "boy's disguise operates not as a liberation but merely as a way of going underground in a difficult situation". Viola is the only Shakespearean heroine who finds it hard to play the part of a man. It prevents her from declaring her love for the duke or even properly defending the capacity of women to love that he denigrates with such self-centred assurance. "Disguise I see thou art a wickedness," she says in Act Two, regarding her "deceit" as a trap from which only time can free her:

What will become of this? As I am man,

CLOTHES

This is a play obsessively concerned with materials and material goods, especially clothes, says Keir Elam. From the straight and unworked flax of Sir An-drew's hair (1.3), to Orsino's emblematic "doublet of changeable taffeta", there are a host of clothes-related images and references. "Even small details of dress, such as the colour of a major-domo's stockings... become in Shakespeare's hands points of actual dramatic importance, and by some of them the action of the play in question is conditioned absolutely," commented Oscar Wilde. Even the manly Sebastian is clothes-conscious,

My state is desperate for my master's love.
As I am woman, now, alas the day,
What thriftless sighs shall poor Olivia breathe!
O time, thou must untangle this, not I.
It is too hard a knot for me t' untie. (2.2)

Later, alarmed by the prospect of playing the "phallic" role of sword-wielding duellist in her confrontation with Sir Andrew, she says in an aside: "A little thing would make me tell them how much I lack of a man" – a clear allusion to her "lack" of manly physical attributes and character. In her essay on cross-dressing on Shakespeare's stage, Jean Howard maintains that because Viola doesn't want to be Cesario, or like being a boy, *Twelfth Night* does not really challenge what she calls the patriarchal gender system: the set of

apologising for being "grossly clad". Clothes are the means by which Viola disguises herself and Olivia, with her veil, conceals herself.

"*Twelfth Night* presents perhaps the most radical vision of the centrality of clothes to the fashioning of a person," say Ann Rosalind Jones and Peter Stallybras. This is especially true of Malvolio, fooled, as he is, into dressing showily against his puritanical principles. By 1600, cross-garters were no longer fashionable, as Maria confirms when she says: "Most villainously, [cross-gartered], like a pedant that keeps a school i'th' church". The joke, says Keir Elam, is that Malvolio, "aspiring to gentrification... succeeds only in associating himself with the lower classes from which he desperately wants to distance himself". Malvolio's cross-dressing is like the negative mirror image of Viola's, as disastrous as hers is successful ■

political constraints, maintained by men, that oppress women. Once she has adopted the disguise she is forced to control her own desires while characters from Orsino to Sir Toby indulge in theirs. And why *should* Viola want to be a boy? It would make no sense to argue that Juliet (in *Romeo and Juliet*) should actually want to be a boy; so why expect this of Viola?

> Despite her masculine attire and the confusion it causes in Illyria, Viola's is a properly feminine subjectivity; and this fact countervails the threat posed by her clothes and removes any possibility that she might permanently aspire to masculine privileges and prerogatives.

Olivia, thinks Howard, with her social and financial independence, is a much bigger threat to the "hierarchical gender system" than Viola is.

Behind the question of sexual ambiguity lies the broader question, which we've already touched on, of what is meant by the word "self". When Feste tells Orsino his tailor should make him a doublet of "changeable taffeta" he suggests that Orsino's moody behaviour has made him inconsistent: his secure sense of self has vanished, leaving a void in its place. But Orsino is not alone in his delusion. What Viola, Orsino and Olivia experience as "the torments of unrequited love and the baffled anguish inflicted by sexual disguise", says Kiernan Ryan, "allows the audience to delight in a world where the illusion of the self's singularity has been dispelled, the customary definitions of masculine and feminine no longer apply, and hard and fast distinctions between the varieties of sexual desire have been dissolved".

When Viola and Olivia meet, there is a telling exchange:

OLIVIA:
  Stay, I prithee tell me what thou think'st of me.
VIOLA:
  That you do think you are not what you are.
OLIVIA:
  If I think so, I think the same of you.
VIOLA:
  Then think you right, I am not what I am. (3.1)

As Ryan points out, Shakespeare chooses the word "are" here, when one might expect him to use the word "seem", and this time in relation not only to the disguised Viola, but to Olivia as well.

The implication is that distinctions between apparent and actual identity simply mask the complexity of the self, which is inherently divided to begin with. The undisguised Olivia is no more self-identical than the Viola veiled by her alter ego and her brother's double, Cesario. And what's true of Olivia is by extension true of the rest of the *dramatis personae,* who are all imposters inasmuch as they are all impersonating themselves. Viola's performance as Cesario is in this sense a metaphor for what all the characters in *Twelfth Night* are up to, whether they adopt a disguise or not: passing themselves off as whoever they are supposed to be by playing parts that don't coincide with them, and thus can't contain them completely. Orsino, Feste, Sebastian, Malvolio, Maria, Sir Andrew: any of them might say like Viola with equal justification: "I am not what I am."

It is through Viola and Sebastian that Shakespeare dramatises most vividly the riddle of the self. As he had shown ten years earlier, in *The Comedy of Errors*, the blueprint for subsequent comedies, one merit of identical twins is that their existence, as Ryan says, "exposes the instability of the identities on which our understanding of people and things relies, and the vulnerability of our minds and senses to deception". Shakespeare deliberately stresses the miraculous quality of the play's denouement, when Orsino sees Sebastian and Cesario together for the first time. "One face, one voice, one habit, and two persons, / A natural perspective, that is and is not" (5.1), Orsino exclaims in amazement. Antonio is equally confounded:

> *How have you made division of yourself?*
> *An apple cleft in two is not more twin*
> *Than these two creatures.*

Sebastian and Viola being reunited in Act V, Scene I of Tim Carroll's 2012 all-male production at The Apollo Theatre

The twins in *Twelfth Night* become, for Shakespeare, an image of the fragmentation of the self – of the way in which, at their core, people are divided into a multitude of different selves.

It is this division, suggests Ryan's fellow Marxist critic, Terry Eagleton, that makes a man or a woman seek to define his or her 'self' in relation to someone else.

To love is to live an imaginary identification with another, so that identity is always at once here and elsewhere, here *because* elsewhere; but if the self is always elsewhere it can err and be misappropriated, plunging you into self-estrangement. If identity is always partly 'other', then one can exert no full control over it; the self is radically 'split' from the outset, a prey to the capricious identifications of those with whom it identifies.

We need to keep two different aspects of our experience of the play in balance. We should not allow our awareness of the characters as individuals to blind us to the structural role of cross-dressing as a mode of challenging assumptions about how men and women behave; on the other hand, concentrating too much on this can lead us to ignore the humanity of the characters about whose lives Shakespeare is writing. Viola as Cesario does indeed raise questions about gender and the nature of the self, and may even suggest there are no *natural* ways for men and women to behave, but we should also recognise the painful quality of *Viola's* desires and the admirable way in which – as a woman – she negotiates her difficult position.

What should we make of Antonio's relationship with Sebastian?

In *Twelfth Night*, Shakespeare takes the two most

powerful forms of desire in his society – sexual love and the desire for social advancement – and crosses them with the two most prevalent forms of difference in personal relationships – gender and social status. In both instances he transgresses established boundaries: servants yearn for masters and sexual desire occurs between members of the same sex.

Antonio's declaration of his love for Sebastian has long caused controversy. Some critics, like Joseph Pequigny and Stephen Orgel, read it as unambiguous homosexual passion; others as an example of the kind of Platonic friendship between men that the philosopher Montaigne celebrates. Nineteenth century directors were so uncomfortable with the first scene between Antonio and Sebastian (2.2) that they often left it out of productions.

Bruce Smith and others have shown that same-sex relationships were viewed quite differently when the play was written to the way they are viewed now. The idea of a natural "sexual orientation" would have been foreign to Shakespeare and his contemporaries, and the concept of "sodomy" (which was illegal) covered a wide range of sexual trespass, not confined to same-sex acts or attraction. It therefore makes little sense to ask whether Antonio is "homosexual" in the modern sense of the term. What we can say, first, is that his devotion to Sebastian is intensely passionate, deeply felt, and selfless. It is very similar to Viola's devotion to Orsino. It drives him to put himself into life-threatening danger for his friend:

I have many enemies in Orsino's court,
Else would I very shortly see thee there.
But come what may, I do adore thee so
That danger shall seem sport, and I will go.
(2.2)

Viola loves her master with an intensity that matches Antonio's desire for Sebastian: "I could not stay behind you. My desire, / More sharp than filèd steel, did spur me forth" (3.5). Just as Viola can be with Orsino only in the form of his dedicated servant, so too Antonio can accompany Sebastian only by switching from friend to servant. (In *Twelfth Night*, service is a condition which makes love, possible.) Finally, both love their masters with dedicated selflessness; they are each prepared to sacrifice themselves for the sake of the loved one, which marks their signal difference from Malvolio, who desires Olivia for his own ambitious reasons. Both embody the ideal of selfless service with the intensity of love.

In this context we should note that, in the fictional world of Illyria, the objects of desire are, except in the case of Malvolio, either apparently or actually of the same sex as the aspirant lovers: Antonio/Sebastian are the pattern for Olivia/Viola and Orsino/Cesario, even if, in the end, these last two turn into heterosexual relationships, with Antonio finally left as an odd man out. Valerie Traub insists on Antonio's exclusion, arguing that the possibility of same-sex desire across the play is quarantined and finally marginalised:

> ...the homoerotic energies of Viola, Olivia and Orsino are displaced on to Antonio, whose relation to Orsino is finally sacrificed for the maintenance of institutionalized heterosexuality and generational continuity.

Like other critics, Traub combines a heavy emphasis on the comedic ending – in which same-sex desire is marginalised – with an assumption about the homogeneity of audience responses. This ignores the fact that the ending does not obliterate our experiences and impressions as we watch the play and are moved by it.

Antonio could be described as Shakespeare's code name for an older man in love with a younger one. In "The Two Antonios and Same-Sex Love in *Twelfth Night* and *The Merchant of Venice*", Joseph Pequigney looks at how much in common there is between the characters in the two plays. "Bisexual experiences are not the exception but the rule in *Twelfth Night*," he says, "and they are vital to the course of love leading to wedlock for the three principal lovers other than Sebastian: Orsino, Olivia and Viola."

Orsino, when he asks for Viola's hand in Act Five, is proposing marriage to someone he has only ever seen as a male servant, whose feminine name he never once utters and whom, during even this scene, he twice addresses as "boy". When, early on, as we've noted, he seems to perceive Viola's true gender, noting her girlish lip and voice "all" as "semblative of a woman's part", Pequigney interprets his response as being a symptom of "homoerotic proclivities". He quotes Freud: "what excited a man's love" in ancient Greece (and still may do so) "was not the masculine character of a boy, but his physical resemblance to a woman as well as his feminine mental qualities", with the "sexual object" being "someone who combines the characters of both sexes". And surely, says Pequigney, Orsino's love

> could not have changed instantaneously with the revelation of [Viola's] femaleness; if it is erotic then it would have been erotic before... This love that commences as homoerotic and conducts Orsino into nuptial heterosexuality is an unbroken curve, a bisexual continuity.

As for Olivia: if she misses the tell-tale signs of femaleness in Viola that Orsino picks up on, that is because "it is in her erotic interest to fantasise Cesario as virile" – yet there is a feminine subtext which is hard to ignore: Olivia has lesbian tendencies. In his last speech to her, Sebastian says, almost tauntingly:

> *So comes it, lady, you have been mistook*
> *But nature to her bias drew in that.*
> *You would have been contracted to a maid;*
> *Nor are you therein, by my life, deceiv'd:*
> *You are betroth'd both to a maid and man. (5.1)*

She has been "mistook" both in taking Cesario for
a man and being captivated by a woman. But in
being "mistook" nature "drew" to "her bias", or
described a curved course (like the curve of a
bowling ball that the noun denotes), and, says
Pequigney, "this homoerotic swerving or lesbian
deviation from the heterosexual straight and
narrow" cannot be considered unnatural since it is
brought about "by nature itself". So like Orsino,
Olivia goes through a homoerotic phase. (Harold
Bloom disagrees: "Olivia's passion is more a
farcical exposure of the arbitrariness of sexual
identity than it is a revelation that mature female
passion essentially is lesbian.") But the most
extreme example of the recurring theme of
bisexuality is Sebastian, who is attracted to both a
man and a woman "who are, and with obvious
passion, enamoured of him".

   In his attempt to, as he puts it, "secure the
homoerotic character of the friendship" between
Antonio and Sebastian, Pequigney points to the
way Antonio continually refers to his passion, both
in their first scene together (as we have noted

above) and later. In the last act, under the mistaken impression Sebastian has refused to return money given him, he rages about his apparently misplaced devotion – "O how vile an idol proves this god..." – and does so with the kind of religious devotion Shakespeare uses in some of his most powerful sonnets:

> *Let not thy love be called idolatry,*
> *Nor my beloved as an idol show... (105)*

There is an ambiguity about the time scheme in *Twelfth Night* – in Act One, scene four, it is stated that "three days" have elapsed since Viola arrived in court, while in the final scene both Antonio and Orsino refer to "three months" having elapsed since the shipwreck. Pequigney uses this to bolster his case:

> ...for months [Sebastian] has continuously remained with an adoring older man who is frankly desirous of him, who showered him with kindnesses [3.4] and who, moreover, saved him from death at sea and nursed him back to health. It is the classic homoerotic relationship, wherein the mature lover serves as guide and mentor to the young beloved.

Pequigney further suggests that Sebastian uses the alias Roderigo to hide his identity during the long drawn-out sexual liaison with a stranger. But that alias could just as well be explained by Sebastian's natural circumspection: he may have been unsure as to whether he could trust Antonio (perhaps because of his suspected piracy). Roger Warren is quite right when he says that Pequigney's arguments do not "secure" the Antonio-Sebastian relationship as homoerotic, though they do underline the way that the text at least *permits* a homoerotic interpretation.

Why does the taunting of Malvolio make us uncomfortable?

Malvolio is *Twelfth Night*'s most ambivalent character – not in what he thinks or feels but in the ways he engages an audience. Graham Holderness says that he may be regarded as the "central figure in the play". That was certainly how the law student Manningham viewed him in 1602, and recent critics like Ivo Kamps have suggested that far from being an outcast, Malvolio may in fact embody the world to come, in which aristocratic exclusivity is challenged by a new, upwardly mobile middle class. Malvolio, along with Feste, is Shakespeare's greatest creation in *Twelfth Night*, says Harold Bloom: "it has become Malvolio's play, rather like Shylock's gradual usurpation of *The*

Merchant of Venice... His dream of socio-economic greatness – 'To be Count Malvolio' – is one of Shakespeare's supreme inventions, permanently disturbing as a study in self-deception, and in the spirit's sickness."

Marxist criticism interprets Malvolio

…as a study in class ideology, but that reduces both the figure and the play. What matters most about Malvolio is not that he is Olivia's household steward but that he so dreams that he malforms his sense of reality, and so falls victim to Maria's shrewd insights into his nature.

Maria is Malvolio's great antagonist: they loathe each other, a "proper match of negative energies". Maria's accurate description of him – "a time pleaser, an affectioned ass... so crammed (as he thinks) with excellencies, that it is his grounds of faith that all that look on him love him" – is one of the most savage in Shakespeare, yet what happens to him is savage too, perhaps disproportionately so.

The clash which triggers Malvolio's unhappy come-uppance occurs in the so-called drinking scene (III.ii) Disturbed by the rowdy, late-night party, Malvolio intervenes, telling off Maria (who, he implies, ought to know better) for indulging such excess, and confronting Sir Toby directly in an intense conflict of wills and values:

My masters, are you mad? Or what are you?
Have you no wit, manners, nor honesty but to
gabble like tinkers at this time of night?... Is there
no respect of place, persons, nor time in you? (2.3)

Cedric Watts suggests that Malvolio's complaint in
fact "makes very good sense". The late-night
revellers are indeed noisy, thoughtless and
besotted. Maria has herself pointed this out just
before his arrival: "What a caterwauling you do
keep here!"

Moreover, Malvolio is acting not on his own
account but as Countess Olivia's dutiful employee:

Sir Toby, I must be round with you. My lady bade
me tell you that, though she harbours you as her
kinsman, she's nothing allied to your disorders...

Sir Toby's famous response – "Dost thou think,
because thou art virtuous, there shall be no more
cakes and ale?" – is preceded by the scornfully
snobbish remark: "Art any more than a steward?"
It's hard not to feel some sympathy for Malvolio
here: Sir Toby is an irresponsible, indulgent
wastrel, who has spent whatever money he might
have had and is living off the good graces of his
niece and the gullibility of his friend, Sir Andrew
Aguecheek. Malvolio is the sober, responsible
servant devoted not only to keeping order in a
household that is ostensibly mourning the dead,
but also to ensure his mistress's economic solvency

– upon which all the other members of the household, including Maria and Sir Toby, depend.

In his essay, "The Audience as Malvolio", Stephen Booth argues that audiences end up sympathising with Malvolio more than they feel they should. For one thing, Sir Toby, though often seen as "a lovable swaggerer, a ne'er-do-well, a bluff, hearty eccentric", is not as amusing as he's assumed or expected to be.

I may indeed be wrong, but – although I surely exaggerate when I imply that nobody ever found Toby funny – I have reason to think not only that my response to Toby is not idiosyncratic but that it is usual.

Audiences faced with Sir Toby often "sound as if they are trying to demonstrate to one another that they are having a very good time" when they aren't. His attempts at wit are strained. "Approach, Sir Andrew. Not to be abed after midnight is to be up betimes; and *diluculo surgere*, thou know'st," he says, to which Sir Andrew's literalistic response – "Nay, by my troth, I know not but I know to be up late is to be up late" – is funnier, largely because it isn't intended to be. Only "an idiot", says Harold Bloom, and "there have been many such", would compare "this fifth-rate rascal to Shakespeare's great genius, Sir John Falstaff".

The result of the noisy and not very witty revels, Booth argues, is that by the time "Malvolio the spoilsport" enters to try and stop them "we the audience – firmly and forever allied with the forces of free-spirited good fellowship – feel something different from, but uncomfortably akin to, sympathy with Malvolio's point of view". The revellers aren't worthy of us; they're not funny enough; we cheer them on, but "it isn't easy". Or, as Ralph Berry has put it: "There is an all but universal convention for commentators to stand up and be counted as in favour of cakes and ale."

Malvolio, of course, is temperamentally joyless and severe; he represents the anti-comic spirit. "I marvel your ladyship takes delight in such a barren rascal," he says of Feste, and Olivia aptly replies: "O, you are sick of self-love, Malvolio..." It is the disparity between Malvolio's professed correctness on behalf of his mistress and his own deep longing for upward social mobility that evokes anger in Maria, Feste and Sir Toby and prompts them to shame him by exposing that ambition to the ridicule of the very person he desires, Olivia. If erotic desire in this play is portrayed as a form of disease and madness, the Malvolio sub-plot allows Shakespeare to show what the metaphor really means by rendering it literal in Sir Topaz's tormenting of Malvolio's supposed madness.

Does Malvolio deserve the treatment meted out to him? Sir Toby Belch is a "feckless booze-hound", in Kiernan Ryan's phrase, and *Twelfth Night*'s "resident Lord of Misrule", presiding over "an unofficial Feast of Fools", while Sir Andrew's idiocy and profligacy go hand in hand with the love of the bottle he shares with Belch, in whose company "he's drunk nightly" (1.3). In their capering and "unbridled buffoonery", says Ryan, they try and milk language for laughs and lose no opportunity to "let the sex-drive surface in a double entendre". Sir Andrew's hair, Toby assures him, "hangs like a flax on a distaff, and I hope to see a housewife take thee between her legs and spin it off" (1.3). As their surnames, Aguecheek and Belch, suggest:

SIR ANDREW

Even though Sir Toby is Olivia's uncle and a knight, he is virtually penniless, and is therefore in social decline. To sustain his dissolute lifestyle, Sir Toby not only has to live off Olivia, he also needs to keep Sir Andrew gulled with assurances of his marriage prospects with Olivia so that Toby is assured of a supply of ready cash, which he is not getting from his niece.

Once Sir Andrew ceases to be of any use to Toby, the knight reveals his real contempt for the poor gull: "An ass-head and a coxcomb and a knave, a thin-faced knave, a gull" (5.1).

There are several hints that as well as emasculated financially he is also infertile, even impotent. Maria jokes that "now I let go your hand I am barren" (1.3); Sir Toby talks of his lank hair, reminiscent of Chaucer's Pardoner: "it hangs like a distaff". Sir Andrew himself is reluctant to use his masculine weapon in the duel with the equally reluctant, unmasculine Cesario ∎

the body calls the shots [in this carnival comedy], giving free rein to urges and appetites that are usually curbed, letting gratification ride roughshod over obligation. In this inverted world, where what you will, not what you should, is the motto, the repressed returns to take revenge on the forces of repression, playing fast and loose with the principles and protocols of civil society. Normal values are reversed: recklessness is prized over sobriety; sense surrenders to nonsense, folly becomes wisdom and wisdom becomes folly; materialism trumps morality; and *carpe diem* rather than *contemptus mundi* is the only creed that counts.

In the confrontation between the revellers and Malvolio, Shakespeare is staging the conflict between the unbridled dramatic imagination epitomised by *Twelfth Night* and the forces of Puritanism and rectitude which were to close the theatres at the start of the Civil War in 1642. Maria says of Malvolio when he storms off that "sometimes he is a kind of Puritan", though it is later carefully stressed that this Puritanism may be purely opportunistic. ("The dev'l a puritan that he is, or anything constantly but a time pleaser" (1.3).)

What better way to humiliate Malvolio – this "poe-faced foe of roistering" – than by exploiting his infatuation with himself? As Ryan says, Maria's clever ruse inveigles Malvolio into precisely the kind of behaviour he condemns: taking liberties and displaying "no respect for place, persons, nor time" in his speech, dress and manner. On picking up the forged letter, he notices the handwriting, which he attributes to Olivia, and unconsciously cracks an obscene joke at her expense:

> *By my life, this is my lady's hand. These be her very c's, her u's and her t's, and thus makes she her great P's (2.5).*

Sir Andrew, typically, doesn't get the joke, with its reference not only to Olivia's "cut" (in Elizabethan slang the word had no 'n' in it) but to her peeing copiously. Malvolio thus turns into a travesty of himself, acting in a way which will encourage the very "uncivil rule" he has denounced in Sir Toby.

Our sympathy for Malvolio, whose name means "ill-will" or "malevolence", must at this stage be limited. Some critics, like Ralph Berry, identify the scene as the moment when audiences start to become uneasy. But the forces of literary tradition and folk culture are on Sir Toby's side. The carousers represent the spirit of carnival and the theatre itself against that of realism and sobriety. "To see the self-destruction of a person who cannot laugh, and hates laughter in others, becomes an experience of joyous exuberance for an audience that is scarcely allowed time to reflect upon its own aroused sadism," says Harold Bloom. Carried away by supposedly amorous hints in

Olivia's faked letter, Malvolio's rhapsodic outburst, as he imagines his grand future, is both funny and disturbing, his egoism and vanity reflected in a succession of "I"s. "I will be proud, I will read politic authors, I will baffle Sir Toby, I will wash off gross acquaintance..." Perhaps we "shudder" a bit as we laugh, says Bloom.

> The erotic imagination is our largest universal, and our most shameful, in that it must turn upon our overvaluation of the self as object. Shakespeare's uncanniest power is to press perpetually upon the nerve of the erotic universal. Can we hear this, or read this, without to some degree becoming Malvolio?

The scene in which Feste, disguised as the Chaucerian curate, Sir Topaz, tries to drive Malvolio into believing that he is mad has been the subject of much controversy. Some believe that even here the kill-joy Malvolio gets what he deserves, others that there is a point where the joke goes too far – that there is something indescribably cruel, something that goes to the core of our anxieties about being treated as mad when one is not. The scene reaches towards the deepest levels of human powerlessness and vulnerability. It is with some relief, then, that Sir Toby himself suggests that the prank were best ended:

I would we were well rid of this knavery. If he

may be conveniently delivered, I would he were,
for I am now so far in offence with my niece that I
cannot pursue with any safety this sport the
upshot. (4.2)

Among those who think Malvolio is justly
punished is Barbara Lewalski, who writes:

> Since he so richly deserves his exposure, and so
> actively cooperates in bringing it upon himself,
> there seems little warrant for the critical tears
> sometimes shed over his harsh treatment and
> none at all for a semi-tragic rendering of his
> plight in the "dark house".

For C.L. Barber, Malvolio is "a kind of foreign body
to be expelled by laughter, in Shakespeare's last
free-and-easy festive comedy". It may be easier
and pleasanter for us, as for these critics, to
pretend that Malvolio gets his just deserts, but
does he? Ralph Berry argues that it is
sentimentalising *Twelfth Night* to see Malvolio as
a tragic figure, but finds something shrill in the
critical responses which hold that he is treated
fairly. Shakespeare built into the design of his play
"a threat to its own mood", maintaining that "the
ultimate effect of *Twelfth Night* is to make the
audience ashamed of itself".

In a play full of lonely, questing individuals,
lacking fathers, sisters, brothers and indeed
mothers, Malvolio is the loneliest, trapped in a

loveless solitude, unable, as the other putative lovers are, to form any real attachment, a predicament reflected in his punishment. "Shakespeare's Malvolio is perpetually trapped in the dark house of his obsessive self-regard and moral censoriousness," writes Harold Bloom.

This is dreadfully unfair, but in the madness of *Twelfth Night*, does that matter? There can be no answer when Malvolio complains to Olivia that he has been "made the most notorious geck [butt] and gull / That e'er invention play'd on", and asks: "Tell me why?"

Certainly the last scenes in *Twelfth Night* call for conflicting responses. After the tormenting of Malvolio, the theme of madness remains, though taken up in a very different way in the very next scene when Sebastian, caught by a deliriously amorous Olivia who mistakes him for his twin sister, marvels at the world in which he now finds himself:

This is the air; that is the glorious sun.
This pearl she gave me, I do feel 't and see 't.
And though 'tis wonder that enwraps me thus,
Yet 'tis not madness. (4.3)

This is an apt description of the wonder of the state of love, but equally of the madness of the play-world itself, of which the supposed realist,

Malvolio, bears the brunt. The darkness into which he is dumped has its counterpart in Sebastian's wonder at the reality of the air and the sun.

Does Feste embody the spirit of *Twelfth Night*?

Feste can almost be seen as an embodiment of Shakespeare's theatre. His ability to turn words inside out, to release unexpected meaning through puns, and his assumption of a popular voice of wisdom through his songs calls into question settled notions of authority, of what is natural, and what is proper. That is in part why Feste spends so much time with Sir Toby, Maria, Fabian and Sir Andrew.

But Feste is more than just a truth-teller, or the embodiment of a literary tradition; he is also a character in a Jacobean household. Olivia's father's fool, he now keeps a caring eye on her. But he is not confined to that household. When we first meet him, Maria threatens him with their mistress's displeasure because he has been out without permission. We soon discover that he has been freelancing at the duke's court, where his melancholic love songs are in great demand. Such movement allows him as much flexibility as he produces from the words he turns inside out, and affords him the opportunity to cadge extra cash with his wit: "always consciously a dependent, [he is] a hack with a spiritual life," says the playwright Simon Gray. After his death-wish song in 2.4, Orsino pays him:

ORSINO:
    There's for thy pains.
FOOL:
    No pains, sir. I take pleasure in singing, sir.
ORSINO:
    I'll pay thy pleasure, then.
FOOL:
    Truly, sir, and pleasure will be paid, one time
    or another.
ORSINO:
    Give me now leave to leave thee.
FOOL:
    Now the melancholy god protect thee, and the
    tailor make thy doublet of changeable taffeta,
    for thy mind is a very opal. I would have men
    of such constancy put to sea, that their
    business might be everything and their intent
    everywhere…

Feste not only turns the conventional notion of work or service as pain back on the giver; he also comments in an extraordinary impertinent way on the duke's character or temperament – suggesting in his references to the duke's "melancholy", his putative "changeable taffeta doublet", and the reference to inconstant seafarers whose business and intent are promiscuous, that, contrary to the duke's view of himself as an absolutely constant lover, Orsino is in fact unreliable and changeable. When he turns from the second person "thee" and "thy" (familiar pronouns that signal a lack of proper politeness), to the third person "men of such constancy", Feste seems to be addressing not the duke, but the audience in a sly aside. As an "allowed fool" in the household he can say things to his superiors that no one else would dare to say. He can also address the audience as if he were one of them.

Even *Twelfth Night*'s most generally admired character, Viola, does not escape his censure. He treats her with some disdain and distrust, having seen what must seem questionable behaviour in both Olivia's household and the court. (He may even have penetrated her disguise: "Now Jove in his next commodity of hair send thee a beard" (3.1).) Asked by Viola what he cares for he says:

> *I do care for something. But in my conscience, sir, I do not care for you. If that be to care for nothing, sir, I would it would make you invisible. (3.1)*

Nevertheless, Viola is clever and knowing enough to recognise his value: "This fellow is wise enough to play the Fool..."

The paradox is at the heart of *Twelfth Night*. Feste, though a professional Fool, is the most astute commentator on the play of which he is a part. Harold Bloom believes that everyone in the play "except the reluctant jester, Feste, is essentially mad without knowing it". *Twelfth Night* is full of characters who deceive themselves and/or others, so much so that, as Keir Elam says in his introduction to the Arden edition of *Twelfth Night*, interpretation itself – making sense of other people's dress, or letters, or actions – is a key theme:

> ...much of the play's action is taken up with the attempt to decipher impenetrable texts (in the form of letters), bodies (notably Viola's), hearts (Orsino's, Olivia's, Cesario's) and events (such as the shipwreck and its consequences). It is a play "about" interpretation as well as a play that has received more than its share of interpretations.

Feste highlights or foregrounds this impenetrability in his riddling and word-play, raising a question which resounds throughout the play: "who is the true fool (or, indeed, are we all fools)?" His role in a world in which, as he puts it, "Foolery... shines everywhere" is not so much to play the fool as to reveal the follies of others.

Talking to Viola, he describes himself to her as "a corrupter of words": it is an important exchange, much of it concerning the limitations and elusiveness of language. Feste's first joke – a play on the word "by" which can mean either "beside" or "by means of" – is typical.

> VIOLA:
> *Dost thou live by the tabor?*
> FESTE:
> *No, sir, I live by the church. (3.1)*

Feste mocks the age in which they live as one where:

> *A sentence is but a cheveril glove to a good wit; how quickly the wrong side may be turned outward!*

Viola answers playfully:

> *They that dally nicely with words may quickly make them wanton.*

FOOLS

During the medieval and early modern periods kings and members of the nobility kept fools as entertainers. Their traditional dress was "motley", a multi-coloured uniform topped by a fool's cap, usually with three differently coloured points with bells attached to them, and a stick (called a bauble) to which was attached either a fool's head or a bag filled with sand.

Shakespeare's plays contain many well-known fools. Most prominent are those in *King Lear*, *As You Like It*, and *Twelfth Night*. The fool's parts were probably written

She means that ingenious word play can render language ambiguous, but Feste responds to the sexual connotations in "dally" and "wanton", and proceeds to link words with names: "I would therefore my sister had had no name, sir" for "her name's a word, and to dally with that word might make my sister wanton". His reaction is typical of the way he plays subtly on the relationship between words and things. As a "corrupter of words", he continually breaks the intended bond between the 'signifier' (a word or name) and the 'signified' (what it's intended to represent).

By exposing the instability of language, he exposes, too, the instability of the world as we know it, or believe it to be. "The labile nature of language," says Kiernan Ryan, "is immediately linked to the wilfulness of the libido by the quip about making words wanton, which identifies wordplay in *Twelfth Night* as indivisible from the

to accommodate the talents of Robert Armin, an actor who joined the company at about the time *Twelfth Night* was written, and who was particularly adept at witty repartee rather than the traditional skills of tumbling and juggling. Such a fool who entertains and is entertained by his wit is, as Olivia puts it, an "allowed fool" – that is to say, he was given free rein to say and do things that were beyond the social and political bounds of members of the court or household. He is the voice not only of humour but also of satire, mockery, and social correction. To Malvolio's contemptuous criticism of Olivia's Fool, she responds: "There is no slander in an allowed Fool, though he do nothing but rail; nor no railing in a known discreet man, though he do nothing but reprove" (1.5) ∎

comedy's demonstration that gender is a fluid concept and sexual desire ungovernable." Feste often hints at how we pretend to know things, citing invented Latin authorities – "For what says Quinapalus? 'Better a witty fool than a foolish wit'" (1.v) – and talks in riddles. He makes pseudo-philosophical affirmations of a tautological nature – "That that it is... for what is 'that' but 'that' and 'is' but 'is'?" – and in effect suggests that language, like human identities, is inherently unstable and slippery and that, in fact, *we really know nothing at all*: "Nothing that is so is so" (4.1).

The whole thrust of his discourse is to subvert meaning. He sees language as quite inadequate to its task, while acknowledging that we are dependent on it:

FESTE:
But indeed, words are very rascals, since bonds disgraced them.
VIOLA:
Thy reason, man?
FESTE:
Troth, sir, I can yield you none without words, and words are grown so false. I am loath to prove reason with them.

It is the view that Nietzsche expressed 300 years later: language traps and falsifies reality. But while words may distort meaning they're the only means we have to make ourselves understood. And for all

the games he plays, Feste is capable of using words
with admirable directness, as his songs – the part
was written for Robert Armin, who had a beautiful
voice – eloquently testify. In his first song, he
expands on the advice he has earlier given to Viola,
to gather rosebuds while she may:

> What is love? 'Tis not hereafter,
> Present mirth hath present laughter.
> What's to come is still unsure.
> In delay there lies no plenty,
> Then come kiss me, sweet and twenty.
> Youth's a stuff will not endure.

When Feste sings this in Trevor Nunn's film of
Twelfth Night, Maria, Andrew and Toby are drawn
into a poignant moment as they reflect on the loss
of youth and pleasure: they are suddenly
confronted by their own precariousness – by the
slipping away of the pleasures and pains of youth.
Feste's second song is similarly straightforward,
though grimmer: the singer, wasted by unfulfilled
longing, expects and wishes for death.

> Come away, come away death,
>   And in sad cypress let me be laid.
> Fie away, fie away breath,
>   I am slain by a fair cruel maid. (2.4)

Feste goes on to sing of the "shroud of white" in the
"black coffin", making them sound so alluring that

the desire for the "fair cruel maid" seems to contain within it a plea for annihilation and oblivion.

Feste's final song, sung as an epilogue, is in the same melancholic vein:

> *When that I was and a little tiny boy,*
> *With hey, ho, the wind and the rain,*
> *A foolish thing was but a toy,*
> *For the rain it raineth every day.*

H.C. Goddard thinks the song

> puts the keystone in place and sums it all up. The thing that this society of pleasure-seekers has forgotten is the wind and the rain. It's all right to play with toys while we are children, and later we may thrive for a little time by swaggering or crime. But knaves and thieves are soon barred out. There is such a thing as coming to a man's estate, such a hard reality.

Feste thus closes the play with an ironic commentary on the happiness of the comic ending, reminding us that human beings have an infinite capacity for foolishness, recklessness, pride, humiliation and violence. The "foolish thing", usually taken to mean the male member, is, amidst all this just "a toy" in "Man's estate".

Opposite: Stephen Fry as Malvolio in Twelfth Night *at The Apollo Theatre, London, 2012*

Of course, we should not take what Feste says completely at face value. Just as the festival recklessness of Sir Toby and company is out of touch with the cold realities of the real world of hard work and suffering, and Orsino's fantasy of love does not match any real person, the cynicism expressed in the song is not quite accurate either. The rain may rain often enough, especially in England, but it does not quite rain every day.

The strain of bitterness in Feste complicates our feelings towards him. Kiernan Ryan points out that the protagonists of Shakespeare's tragedies, including the more or less contemporary *Hamlet*, share with him a sense of estrangement from the world "so complete that apparent nonsense alone makes sense, because what the world considers sensible is plainly insane". Harold Bloom calls

WORD PLAY

Certain words and ideas crop up repeatedly in *Twelfth Night*. Stephen Booth has listed them: "music, glut- tony, disease, hunting (in a recurring concern for finding people and in a complex alliteration of various ideas of following), dogs, payment (of debts and for services), sibling relationships (of course), the word alone (and its significances and its etymological roots and their signficances), achieved or frustrated entrance, the sea, seeing, and onstage judgements of onstage performances".

To take two examples from this list: the plotters in the letter scene refer constantly to blood sports (woodcock-

Feste "benign" but Simon Gray's view, that there is in him the malice "of a man who cannot tolerate others knowing what he knows about himself", is perhaps closer to the truth. He "enjoys tormenting Malvolio, whose cold insights ('I marvel your ladyship takes delight in such a tavern rascal... unless you laugh and minister to him, he's gagged') constitute a real threat to his powers of enchantment, and thus to his vanity" and he "crows" over Malvolio when he has been released after his humiliation. Malvolio, as we've seen, *is* "most notoriously abused" and we shouldn't forget that it is the Fool, witty, eloquent and musical as he is, who, in the guise of Sir Topaz, most abuses him.

The source of Feste's melancholy is never explained, though his haunting songs hint that he has been hurt. (There is a similar suggestion of this

trapping, badger-hunting and bear-baiting), culminating in Malvolio's parting curse: "I'll be revenged on the whole pack of you!" Seeing, or eyes, is a constant theme in a play where how we see things is a constant theme: "O, when my eyes did see Olivia first," says Orsino in the opening scene; Cesario's qualities "creep in at my eyes" (1.5), says Olivia herself; Cesario recounts how "methought her eyes had lost her tongue" (2.2); Sebastian, amazed by Olivia's amorous-ness, says: "I am ready to distrust mine eyes." (4.3).

Booth also notes the subtle use of verbal harmonies in the play which we may not be conscious of but which are part of the play's overall effect. A good example is the word "cat". Within a 20-line passage in 2.3, the cat in Sir Andrew's "I am a dog at a catch" is echoed in Maria's entrance line: "What a caterwauling you do keep here" and Sir Toby's "My lady's a Cataian" ∎

about Sir Andrew in his most famous line: "I was adored once too" (2.3).) "There runs through all [Feste] says and does that vein of irony by which we may so often mark one of life's self-acknowledged failures," says the editor and critic Granville Barker. But Feste, as he reminds us that death shadows the brief delights of love, reflects and embodies a strain of melancholy which runs through the play from the beginning: Orsino's langourous coupling of desire with disease and death is contagious. "The feeling that *Twelfth Night* is an elegy for comedy itself is insistent and inseparable from the strange sadness that suffuses it," says Kiernan Ryan. Viola's love seems as hopeless as Orsino's and Olivia's.

> *How will this fadge? My master loves her dearly,*
> *And I, poor monster, fond as much on him,*
> *And she, mistaken, seems to dote on me. (2.2)*

Viola's desperate state makes her as "addicted to melancholy" (2.5) as Olivia and Orsino, and when Orsino bemoans the transience of female beauty – "women are as roses, whose fair flower / Being once displayed, doth fall that very hour" – Viola echoes him:

> *And so they are. Alas that they are so:*
> *To die even when they to perfection grow. (2.4)*

Who does Orsino want to kill?

After Feste's taunting of Malvolio and the sudden deviation from comic high-spirits to real injury in the mock duel that becomes a real fight, *Twelfth Night* swerves towards its comedic ending. Sebastian is collared by Olivia, seduced and then married before he knows it in a swirl of bewildered fantasy that elaborates on the notion of desire as madness. His sense of wonder at the events that have befallen him will be extended in the final scene, but before that happens, Shakespeare makes us feel the closeness of madness and desire, even to the point of death.

Act Five opens with the confrontation between Antonio, who has sacrificed himself to his enemies to rescue (as he thinks) his beloved Sebastian from danger, and Orsino, the ruler of the state that has declared him an outlaw and pirate. That confrontation rehearses the suppressed sense of violence and violation at love's betrayal that also lurks in the names Viola, Olivia and Malvolio. Believing that Cesario and Sebastian are the same person, Antonio accuses the young man of betraying him, with a bitter intensity unmatched (up to that point) anywhere else in the play:

> *A witchcraft drew me hither.*
> *That most ingrateful boy there by your side*

From the rude sea's enraged and foamy mouth
Did I redeem; a wrack past hope he was.
His life I gave him and did thereto add
My love, without retention or restraint,
All his in dedication. For his sake
Did I expose myself, pure for his love,
Into the danger of this adverse town;
Drew to defend him when he was beset;
Where, being apprehended, his false cunning
(Not meaning to partake with me in danger)
Taught him to face me out of his acquaintance
And grew a twenty years' removèd thing
While one would wink; denied me mine own

purse,

Which I had recommended to his use
Not half an hour before. (5.1)

This is the most intense and moving expression of
love in *Twelfth Night*, given freely and without
"retention of restraint"; the lover, Antonio, is even
prepared to sacrifice his life. The most striking
quality of his expression of love is its proximity to
pure hatred, as "love, without retention or
restraint" is transformed into "a twenty year
removed thing". As Antonio recounts the
ingratitude and betrayal of the young man for
whom he risked everything, his passionate desire
turns to loathing. Such perceived fickleness echoes
Orsino's earlier pronouncements on the inherent
unreliability of women in love, but it also rehearses
the assumed fickleness of young men.

The issue as it applies to Cesario appears to be resolved when it is revealed that the person Antonio accuses of betraying him has been the duke's constant companion for three months. But immediately, on Olivia's entrance, the scene of apparent betrayal and deception is repeated – and intensified. Cesario is now accused (by the countess) of betraying *her*. With the new perception of betrayal, the passions of hatred and violence that underlie sexual desire are unleashed.

Orsino, too, feels betrayed – by Olivia – and it is worth looking at the exchange in which, confronted and rebuffed by Olivia in person, Orsino's thoughts turn from desire to murder and he suddenly begins to sound like Othello:

> Why should I not, had I the heart to do it,
> Like to th' Egyptian thief at point of death,
> Kill what I love? – a savage jealousy
> That sometime savors nobly. But hear me this:
> Since you to nonregardance cast my faith,
> And that I partly know the instrument
> That screws me from my true place in your favor,
> Live you the marble-breasted tyrant still.
> But this your minion, whom I know you love,
> And whom, by heaven I swear, I tender dearly,
> Him will I tear out of that cruel eye
> Where he sits crownèd in his master's spite. –
> Come, boy, with me. My thoughts are ripe in
> mischief.
> I'll sacrifice the lamb that I do love

This exchange between Orsino, Olivia and Viola is the most significant and powerful in the play. The whole comedy has been moving to this sudden eruption of violent hatred: from the invocation of love as a hunt in the opening scene to the repeated instances of loss and mourning for brothers (one dead, another apparently so); the invocation of death in Feste's plangent love songs ("Come away, come away death"); Viola's fictitious sister who is supposed to have died of love; Antonio's readiness to risk death for Sebastian ("If you will not murder me for my love, let me be your servant"); the parody of violently directed passion in the duel scene, followed by real injury when Sebastian appears; and the mutual, explicit animosity in the encounter between Antonio and Orsino and his servant, Cesario. The ground on which the relation between death and desire is elaborated throughout the play lies in its echoes of the story of Narcissus who, in love with his own image, pines away to extinction.

The final scene collects all the complex intensities of love and its relation to hatred, violence and madness that the play has gradually been revealing to us and focuses them in Orsino, its most obvious – but not only – figure of Narcissistic desire.

Confronted by the woman he thinks he loves – this is the first time they talk to each other – only to be repelled by her absolute rejection, Orsino's desires turn murderous: "Why should I not kill what I love?" Whom does he want to kill? The person he loves, of course. *If I can't have you, nobody else will…* But whom does he love? He's been professing his love for Olivia to such excess that the answer seems obvious: he wants to kill Olivia. But he does not. Instead he latches on to Cesario, his faithful servant, dragging him off to "murder [him] for [his] love". Believing that Cesario had encouraged Olivia to fall in love with him (Cesario), Orsino is consumed with anger at the betrayal by his servant, who was supposed to be acting on his behalf.

Orsino may, however, be on the verge of recognising *Cesario* is in fact the one he loves, and has loved all along. Stephen Greenblatt, following the image of the way in which a bowling ball changes its course to hit the jack (or target) through its bias, has suggested that love reaches its goal only by swerving. The swerve in this case is Orsino's recognition – *through his homicidal desire* – that he loves Cesario, *not* Olivia. True love is revealed in a moment of blind hatred.

The swerve allows Viola for the first time to declare her love openly for her master:

VIOLA:
>   *And I, most jocund, apt, and willingly,*
>   *To do you rest a thousand deaths would die.*
OLIVIA:

107

Where goes Cesario?
VIOLA:
After him I love
More than I love these eyes, more than my life,
More by all mores than e'er I shall love wife.

Viola's passion, which echoes, in its intensity,
Antonio's earlier declaration of selfless devotion to
her brother, Sebastian, knows no reservation or
restraint: she is happy to die, to be slaughtered by
the man she loves. Just as Shakespeare always
reminds us of the darkness of emotions, like love,
that we tend to sentimentalise, he reminds us, too,
that the drive for death can be a sign of vitality. In
vowing to Orsino that "I most jocund, apt, and
willingly, / To do you rest a thousand deaths would
die", Viola invokes the Jacobean pun on "death" as
orgasm, declaring both her intense *desire* for her
master and the possibility of her satisfying his
desire – "to do you rest" – through repeated
consummation ("a thousand times").

From this point, having shocked us in its
unexpected turn and violent intensity, the play
moves in a fairly straightforward way to its
resolution. The mistaking of Sebastian for Viola
and Viola for Sebastian is cleared up when Viola's
brother appears, breathless and apologetic for
having injured Olivia's uncle, Sir Toby. There is
another abrupt change of the play's rhythm,
however: the hectic disorder to which the scene
has been building is arrested by the gradual

realisation that Cesario has, impossibly, split in two. On stage this should dawn gradually, in silence, finally broken by the duke's amazement at this miracle: "One face, one voice, one habit, and two persons! / A natural perspective, that is and is not!" The twins enact a moving, wondrous recognition and restoration after each has thought the other dead. In contrast to the turbulent sexually-driven passions which have engaged us up to now, the recognition is especially telling for its reticent wonder, its gradual dawning of belief as they exchange mutual experiences, and its tenderness:

SEBASTIAN:
> *Do I stand there? I never had a brother,*
> *Nor can there be that deity in my nature*
> *Of here and everywhere. I had a sister,*
> *Whom the blind waves and surges have*
> > *devoured.*
> *Of charity, what kin are you to me?*
> *What countryman? What name? What*
> > *parentage?*

VIOLA:
> *Of Messaline. Sebastian was my father.*
> *Such a Sebastian was my brother too.*
> *So went he suited to his watery tomb.*
> *If spirits can assume both form and suit,*
> *You come to fright us.*

SEBASTIAN:
> *A spirit I am indeed,*

But am in that dimension grossly clad
Which from the womb I did participate.
Were you a woman, as the rest goes even,
I should my tears let fall upon your cheek
And say "Thrice welcome, drownèd Viola."

In a play that focuses so intensely on love, here is a still, miraculous moment of real, mutual love – in all its vulnerability, its overcoming of loss and hope of restoration, and its gradual, suspension of disbelief and recognition that one's identity is completely tied up, not in oneself, but in the other person whom one loves. It is a deeply moving moment.

It makes its mark on the duke, who is now able fully and publicly to recognise his love for his servant. He does so by freeing 'him' from service and proposing marriage to 'her':

Your master quits you; and for your service
done him,

DEATH AND DISEASE

Twelfth Night is much preoccupied with death, prompting Frederick Furnivall to note the "shadow of death and distress across the sunshine" in the play. There are also constant references to disease. The word "sicken" occurs in the play's third line and recurs in the exchange about hunting (with "purged" and "pestilence"); Sir Andrew's name, like his gaunt appearance and lank, yellow hair, suggests sickness; the urine of the "distempered" Malvolio, meanwhile, is to be

So much against the mettle of your sex,
So far beneath your soft and tender breeding,
And since you called me "master" for so long,
Here is my hand. You shall from this time be
Your master's mistress.   (5.1)

Orsino's sudden turning from Olivia to Viola, recognising Viola as the person he has loved all along, means that the repressed erotic desire that always ran as an undercurrent in the relationship between master and servant now surfaces as an acknowledged force. The intensity of Orsino's passion has been brought out by the violence of his "thoughts" against Viola/Cesario, and the intensity of her passion has been revealed by her masochistic readiness to die for him and by him. Orsino's desire to kill the thing he loves reveals to him *whom* he actually loves. Comedy achieves its darkest reaches here, but also its moment of greatest clarity.

Orsino's offer to Viola, and his statement that

analysed for signs of disease. "The language of disease beomes general currency for interpersonal relations in the play, above all through the metaphor of contagion," says Keir Elam. Sebastian warns Antonio that "the malignancy of my fate might perhaps distemper yours" (2.1); Malvolio has "taken the infection" of Maria's plot (3.4); Feste has "contagious breath", which reminds us of the most recurrently evoked illness in the play, the deadly bubonic plague. "What a plague means my niece to take the death of her brother thus?" says Sir Toby (1.3); "Even so quickly may one catch the plague?" says Olivia of her sudden falling in love (1.5) ∎

she will from this moment be his "master's mistress", recalls another Shakespeare sonnet:

> A woman's face with nature's own hand painted,
> Hast thou, the master mistress of my passion;
> A woman's gentle heart, but not acquainted
> With shifting change, as is false women's fashion:
> An eye more bright than theirs, less false in rolling,
> Gilding the object whereupon it gazeth;
> A man in hue all hues in his controlling,
> Which steals men's eyes and women's souls amazeth.
> And for a woman wert thou first created;
> Till Nature, as she wrought thee, fell a-doting,
> And by addition me of thee defeated,
> By adding one thing to my purpose nothing.
> But since she prick'd thee out for women's pleasure,
> Mine be thy love and thy love's use their treasure.
> (Sonnet 20)

This is one of Shakespeare's most intriguing poems. Addressed to a beautiful young man, it praises him for being more beautiful than a woman, while nonetheless being characterised by a peculiar feminine beauty. He is more reliable and constant than female fickleness (recall Orsino's denigration of the trustworthiness of women); and, in a peculiar twist, the sonnet argues that the admired young man was in fact first created as a woman by Nature, who (herself a woman) fell in

love with her creation and changed "her" into a
"him", adding only one thing (*"pricked* thee out")
to this epitome of beauty. Addressed to the "master
mistress of my passion", the sonnet offers an
androgynous figure of desire that combines both
male and female qualities.

The most striking thing about the ending of
Twelfth Night is not the fact that its happy double
celebration of marriage excludes a number of
characters who cannot be accommodated fully
within its happy recovery and restoration: Sir Toby
and Maria, Sir Andrew Aguecheek, Malvolio, and
even Feste. It is the fact that Viola remains Cesario
to the end:

> Cesario, come,
> For so you shall be while you are a man.
> But when in other habits you are seen,
> Orsino's mistress, and his fancy's queen.

How significant is it that Viola remains Cesario?
Orsino continues to address her by her assumed
name as male servant, and declares that he will
remain so until the woman's clothes that are in the
Captain's possessions are recovered. That means
that we as spectators will never see Cesario
restored to Viola. The play ends before that can
happen, which means that, for us, Viola remains
Cesario, the selfless, loving, androgynous servant,
whose love, no longer confined to silence, is
reciprocated by the master. Furthermore,

Malvolio, who appears to have banished himself from the happy resolution in which "Golden time convents", returns in an unexpected but crucial way. The sea captain, who has Viola's "woman's weeds" and can confirm her story, has been detained at Malvolio's charge, and presumably cannot be released without Malvolio's willing intervention.

Where does Shakespeare leave us at the end of *Twelfth Night*?

The play ends, as it began, with the invocation of fancy – imagination, delusion, madness, love. What we are promised is, some time in the future, Viola becoming Orsino's "fancy's queen". It is precisely the position that Olivia occupied at the beginning of the play. The play thus leaves us on a strange, troubling threshold: the wondrous realisation by Orsino that Viola is the one he has always loved; Viola's release into being able to "tell her love"; and the disturbing question of whether Viola can live up to Orsino's expectations, and he to hers. The characters are left in a state of what Kiernan Ryan calls "elated anticipation": whether they finally find happiness or disappointment is left uncertain.

We began with the judgment that with *Twelfth Night* Shakespeare not only masters but also *exhausts* the genre of Romantic comedy. What does that mean? It means that while the play draws us into the promise of a "Golden time" at the end, in which conflicts have been reconciled, desires fulfilled, and losses restored, especially through the celebratory closure of marriage, there are too many uncertainties at the *heart* of those achievements (not just as "loose ends") to convince us, emotionally as well as intellectually, of the play's "happy ending".

Twelfth Night shows us both the corrosiveness and the vitality of passionate love, and the violent hatred that is twinned with it. Critics in the 20th century tended to take the happy ending at face value and read the trajectory of the plot as a learning curve through which Orsino and Viola come to recognise their true love for each other: they are supposed to achieve "clarification through release". J.R. Brown writes: "in the light of Shakespeare's threefold ideal of love, the contrasts and conflicts of this comedy are resolved like the last inevitable moves of a chess game". For Brown, Shakespeare's threefold ideal of love encompasses "love's wealth", "love's truth" and "love's order".

In a world that is not quite as sanguine about the uncomplicated combination of wealth, truth and order in love, we now see, with the French psychoanalyst and philosopher, Jacques Lacan, that love is always hovering on the edge of disorder, that its wealth depends upon the lack that constitutes desire, and that its truth is always constituted in part by a degree of illusion. We may respond to the notion of Viola as Orsino's "fancy's Queen" with some misgivings, but *Twelfth Night* shows us that there is an element of fantasy in *all* sexual love: we always love, not the *real thing* but to some extent the image of the person that we have projected on to him or her.

The play does not merely show or tell us things: it *engages* us through its music, its language, and the alluring and changing bodies on the stage in a vital but also disconcerting set of imaginative experiences. To be drawn into this world we need to know and be attentive to the mobility of sexual desire, to passionate and even selfless love, to the power of social ambitions and jealousies. Historical knowledge may be useful, but no contextual information can finally fix or determine an interpretation or our experiences of the play. Bruce Smith puts the action of *Twelfth Night* on the imagination and the senses extremely well:

> We are invited to imagine a visual matrix alive with motion, suffused with erotic desire, out of which figures emerge with quickness and volubility, before they are fixed for contemplation by the understanding.

Guides like this one inevitably are concerned with "fixing" literary works for "contemplation in the understanding". But part of our understanding of *Twelfth Night* should be an appreciation of how little is actually "fixed" – how much moves between joy and sadness, recovery and loss, freedom and restraint, laughter and melancholy, desire and death.

THE CRITICS ON
TWELFTH NIGHT

"A Janus-faced play which looks back to the farcical and festive romantic comedies that preceded it, and forward to the darker, disenchanted vision of the problem plays and the romances' miraculous, bittersweet tales of shipwreck, grief and kindred reunited."
Kiernan Ryan

"For both Orsino and Olivia, self-deception serves as an avoidance of the real world and of real emotion." **David Lewis**

"Viola redeems the play because she proves to be selfless, not selfish, in love. She becomes Echo instead of Narcissus." **Jonathan Bate**

"An abyss hovers just beyond *Twelfth Night*, and one cost of not leaping into it is that everyone, except the reluctant jester, Feste, is essentially mad without knowing it." **Harold Bloom**

"We enjoy the play so much simply because it is a wish-fulfillment presented so skillfully that we do not notice that our hearts are duping our heads."
C.L. Barber, Shakespeare's Festive Comedy, 1965

A SHORT CHRONOLOGY

1558 Elizabeth I comes to the throne

1564 Shakespeare born in Stratford-upon-Avon

1585 Shakespeare's twins, Hamnet and Judith, born

1594 *Love's Labours Lost*

1595-96 *Romeo and Juliet; A Midsummer Night's Dream*

1596 Hamnet dies

c. 1601 *Twelfth Night* written, probably just before *Hamlet*

1602 February 2nd First recorded performance, in the hall of the Middle Temple. John Manningham, a law student, referred to it in his diary

1616 Shakespeare dies on the 23rd April

1623 Twelfth Night included in the First Folio

1661-63 Samuel Pepys sees Twelfth Night three times, despite initially describing it as a "silly play"

1910 First (silent) film of *Twelfth Night*, directed by Charles Kent

1996 Trevor Nunn's film of *Twelfth Night* starring, among others, Imogen Stubbs, Toby Stephens and Nigel Hawthorne

BIBLIOGRAPHY

Baker, Herschel (ed.), *Twelfth Night*, Signet, 1965

Barber, C.L. *Shakespeare's Festive Comedy,* Princeton, New Jersey, 1972

Belsey, Catherine, 'Disrupting sexual difference: meaning and gender in the comedies', 1985, reprinted in *Alternative Shakespeares*, Drakakis, John (ed.), Methuen, 1992

Berry, Edward, *Shakespeare's Comic Rites*, Cambridge University Press, 1959

Berry, Ralph, Shakespeare's Comedies, Princeton, 1972

Berry, Ralph, 'Twelfth Night: 'The Experience of the Audience', Shakespeare Survey 34, 1981

Bloom, Harold, *Shakespeare: The Invention of the Human*, Penguin, 1998

Booth, Stephen, *Precious Nonsense*, University of California, 1998

Cookson, Linda and Loughrey, Brian (eds.), *Critical Essays on Twelfth Night*, Longman, 1990

Dusinberre, Juliet, *Shakespeare and the Nature of Woman*, London and Basingstoke, 1975

Eagleton, Terry, *William Shakespeare*, Blackwell, 1986

Elam, Keir (ed.), *Twelfth Night*, The Arden Shakespeare, 2008

Frye, Northrop, *A Natural Perspective: The Development of Shakespearean Comedy and Romance*, New York and London, 1965

Garber, Marjorie, *Vested Interests: Cross-Dressing and Cultural Anxiety*, Routledge, 1992

Gray, Simon, 'Morally Superior', New Statesman, August 29, 1969

Greenblatt, Stephen, *Shakespearean Negotiations*, Berkeley, 1988

Howard, Jean, 'Cross Dressing, The Theatre, and Gender Struggle in Early Modern England', *Shakespeare Quarterly*, Vol. 39, 1988

Hutson, Lorna, 'On not being deceived: rhetoric and the body in *Twelfth Night*', Texas Studies in Literature and Language, 38. 1996

Kott, Jan, *Shakespeare Our Contemporary*, Methuen, 1964

Leggatt, Alexander, *The Cambridge Companion to Shakespearean Comedy*, Cambridge University Press, 2002

Leggatt, Alexander, *Shakespeare's Comedy of Love*, Routledge, 1973

Levine, Laura, *Men in Women's Clothing*, Cambridge University Press, 1994

Lindley, David, *Shakespeare and Music,* Arden, 2005

Palfrey, Simon, *Doing Shakespeare*, Methuen Drama, 2011

Pequigney, Joseph, 'The Two Antonios and Same-Sex Love in *Twelfth Night* and *The Merchant of Venice*', English Literary Renaissance, Vol. 22, 2008

Ryan, Kiernan, *Shakespeare's Comedies*, Palgrave Macmillan, 2009

Smith, Bruce, 'Sensing Sexual Strangeness in Twelfth Night', in James Schiffer (ed.), *Twelfth Night, New Critical Essays*, Routledge, 2015

Summers, Joseph, 'The Masks of *Twelfth Night*', 1955, reprinted in Palmer, D.J. (ed.), *Shakespeare: Twelfth Night, A Selection of Critical Essays*, Macmillan, 1972

Traub, Valerie, *Desire and Anxiety: Circulations of Sexuality in Shakespearean Drama*, Routledge, 1992

Warren, Roger and Wells, Stanley (eds.), *Twelfth Night*, Oxford University Press, 1994

Witmore, Michael, *Shakespearean Metaphysics*, Continuum, 2008

INDEX

First published in 2015 by
Connell Guides
Artist House
35 Little Russell Street
London WC1A 2HH

9 8 7 6 5 4 3 2 1

Picture credits:
p.19 © c.Fine/Everett/REX
p. 33 © Granada International/REX
p. 48 © Design Pics Inc/REX
p.49 © Ewing Galloway/REX
p. 63 © Moviestore Collection/REX
p. 71 © Geraint Lewis/REX
p.99 © Alastair Muir/ REX

A CIP catalogue record for this book is available from the British Library.
ISBN 978-1-907776-98-4

Design © Nathan Burton
Assistant Editors:
Katie Sanderson, Paul Woodward and Holly Bruce
Printed and bound in Malaysia

www.connellguides.com